CONTENTS

Dedication

for Stephen, Philip, Becky and Hannah

Introduction

When you have learned to ride and, better still, have your own pony, you will soon discover how wide and varied are the ways in which this particular sport can be followed. If you like competing, you are able to do so; if you want to explore the countryside around your home, a pony enables you to roam further afield; if you want to meet and make friends with people with similar interests, a pony provides an excellent introduction.

Riding can have an attraction for almost any type of personality. The bold and the brave may well end up in the adventurous world of eventing; the disciplined rider may choose dressage or show-jumping; whilst the non-competitive can find infinite pleasure simply by hacking in the woods and lanes of their neighbourhood.

There is no age limit in riding. Very small riders can have just as much fun on very small ponies as their older brothers and sisters on bigger ponies and their parents on horses. What you choose to do on your pony is entirely up to you, and even in a family where everyone rides each member can take part in different horsy activities.

Almost all riders, however, at some time in their riding career, will have a go at mounted games.

The best thing about mounted games as a sport is that they can be tailored to suit the age and ability of the rider as well as the age and ability of the pony. They can be team events or for individuals; they can call for highly developed skills or be enjoyed by beginners. And if it is your ambition to ride at Wembley or Aachen or Badminton, or to ride in the World Cup, the Nations Cup or the Olympic Games, they are an excellent introduction to competitive riding.

Nowadays, gymkhana games are regarded as children's activities. You will find them tacked on to the end of a schedule for a big show in which showing and jumping classes predominate. If you are lucky they will start on time, but very often there are long delays because no equipment can be put in

5

position until earlier classes in the ring have finished and the setting up itself seems to take hours. Parents of leading rein children (who get increasingly fractious) finally give up and go home.

When, in the 'fifties, Prince Philip presented a cup to be awarded by the Pony Club for mounted games, gymkhana activities gained some important recognition. The Prince Philip Cup is still the highest accolade in the gymkhana world. But Pony Club mounted games are team events and limited to riders who have not attained their fifteenth birthday by 1 January in any year. Older riders who want to go on enjoying the fun and skills of gymkhanas must join the Mounted Games Association of Great Britain or hope that there will be a few open gymkhana events at local shows.

Yet, in the eighteenth century, gymkhanas were developed for adults to enjoy. This was in India, in the garrison towns and hill stations where the British Army was based. All sorts of mounted activities were organised to help the soldiers and their families to pass the time, build up morale and generally keep everyone happy so far from home.

Gymkhanas – the word itself is a corruption of the Hindi, *gendkhana*, meaning racket-court, and gymnastics – featured many different kinds of races, often with hurdles to add to the fun. Female riders even carried parasols as they negotiated obstacles!

When they returned to Britain, these intrepid horsemen and women looked back with nostalgia at the jolly times they had enjoyed, and it was not long before someone suggested organising similar activities in the British countryside. Gymkhana games became very popular attractions at garden fêtes and parties.

At this time, they were still part of the grown-ups' riding scene. Even after the Second World War, every local show had open gymkhana events, usually run on a circular track and as often as not over wattle sheep hurdles. The VC race (where the rider had to collect and carry back to the start a 'wounded comrade' – in this case a sack stuffed with straw) and the Gretna Green race (where two riders rode over hurdles hand in hand) were extremely popular, always fast and furious and frequently punctuated by spills.

Children's races, however, were held without hurdles and, as today, generally divided by age. For many young riders at the time, gymkhana games offered almost the only chance of taking part in competitions. Unless they had a jumping pony or, more rarely, a show pony, ordinary riders spent the summer taking part in gymkhanas. One-day events, combined training and hunter trials simply did not exist at a level suitable for them. Working hunter pony classes and polocrosse did not exist at all.

It was inevitable, perhaps, that as the range of competitive classes widened gymkhana games would be relegated to a back seat. At the same time, paradoxically, the variety of gymkhana games has increased, largely due to the Pony Club and the Prince Philip Cup. Those who organise the Pony Club games are always looking for new ideas, especially events which do not require expensive equipment. Eventually, their brainwaves filter through to the enthusiasts who run shows. So when you take part in the gymkhana events at your local show, the games you will play owe more to the Pony Club today than to the far-off gymkhanas in India in the last century.

Part 1

Little Ones and Beginners

Chapter One
Leading-Rein Classes

Small children from horsy families may well have started riding by the time they are three years old. In non-horsy families, the starting age is likely to be six or seven. In either case, for gymkhana games, a seven-year-old is safest on the leading rein. This is because most six- and seven-year-olds rely principally on balance for riding skills, relying for control of the pony on the reins alone. Children of that age, even though they may have spent half their young lives in the saddle, have neither the weight nor the length of leg to be totally in command of a pony. In the excitement of a gymkhana, accidents can easily happen.

In most shows leading-rein classes are confined to children aged eight and under. At this level it is very difficult to devise games which do not favour one age group or another. Bending, for example, will always be won by a handler who can run fast with a pony which leads willingly. Similarly, a race such as Ride and Run or Musical Mats, where the rider has to dismount and run to a mat or the finish, is best for the bigger competitors. The only races where no child has an advantage are the ones which depend on luck – Coloured Corners and Crossing the River, for example – but these, unfortunately, can be boring for both rider and handler.

It follows, therefore, that leading-rein classes can be quite stressful for very young riders, and many a three-year-old ends up being carried from the ring in tears.

One of the simplest games on horseback is Grandmother's Footsteps. It is not the sort of game you will find in a show schedule but it is very popular in riding schools, where instructors like to finish a lesson in a fun way. The rules are uncomplicated: the instructor stands facing the wall at one end of the arena while her pupils line up at the other and start creeping up on her. Every so often, she turns round, hoping to catch one or more of them on the move. If she is successful the culprits have to go back to the beginning. In a confined space, such as an indoor school, the riders can compete off the leading-rein, the game teaching them concentration and control. The children soon learn that gentle pressure on the reins will prove far more effective at halting their ponies than a wild tug.

Games afternoons are sometimes organised by riding schools for their pupils. Here, among friends and in a not too competitive atmosphere, you will learn the rules of such games as Bending, Sock and Bucket, Walking and Trotting Races and a few others where the equipment required is straightforward.

Once you leave the riding school and take the giant step of acquiring a pony of your own, you will almost certainly decide that entering a proper gymkhana, with the chance of winning a rosette, is the next stage in your riding career.

Imagine that it is the Easter holidays – the start of the season – and you have picked up the schedule for a nearby show at your local saddlers. It is always exciting to look through the classes and see which ones you are able to enter.

If you are very much a novice and definitely more confident on the leading rein, stick to the leading-rein events. In the few weeks available to you before the show date it is very unlikely that your riding will have improved so much that you can compete entirely on your own.

So what are you likely to find? Most shows feature a leading-rein best rider class. Although this is not a gymkhana event, it is an excellent preparation for other classes. You will be judged on how you sit, how you hold your reins and how well you and your pony move together. You should be able to manage a rising trot without using the reins, and consequently your pony's mouth in order to maintain your balance. You will not be expected to canter and, because the control of your pony is in the hands of your leader, you can concentrate on sitting up straight and keeping your legs still and your feet in the proper position. Best rider contestants circle the arena in single file, first at a walk, then at a trot and then at a walk again. After that, they are called in and asked to line up. Each rider in turn then gives an individual show, usually a simple figure-of-eight at a trot, before returning to the judge and halting. The rider should salute the judge by removing her right hand from the rein and briefly nodding her head. This indicates that the individual show has been completed.

Some judges ask the riders to perform a simple movement such as dismounting. This is to see how well the rider understands basic riding principles.

When the individual show is over, the rider returns to the line-up and waits while the other competitors do their shows. And when all those have been completed, the riders circle the arena once again, while the judges make up their minds and the steward brings the riders into the centre in order of preference.

To be honest, best rider classes, which are often well supported, can be extremely boring, especially for very young riders. There is a lot of waiting around and not much to do, but they certainly make you think about your riding and can teach you useful lessons in ringcraft, such as not crowding the rider in front of you and keeping alert in front of the judge.

So, when you look at your show schedule, it is worth putting a tick against the leading-rein best rider class.

After that, there are not many classes left that a leading-rein rider may enter. The show pony section may well have a leading-rein class, but unless your pony really is a show pony entering it may well be a waste of time. Presentation is everything in such a class, a fashion parade for both rider and handler. The handler will look incredibly elegant in a smart skirt and jacket, with hat to match. The hatband and buttonhole will be selected to go with the pony's browband and the rider's buttonhole and hair ribbons. The pony will be perfectly plaited, perfectly groomed, and if that is a description of your pony it is

Gaining confidence. This rider may be on the leading rein today but it won't be long before she and her pony are competing on their own.

13

very unlikely you will be allowed to ride him in a gymkhana event.

The chances are, however, that you have a very ordinary pony for whom gymkhana events are just right. So, the next thing you look for in your show schedule is the gymkhana section.

Usually, these are divided into age groups. It is better for everybody if leading-rein classes are separated from the others as there are few classes where led and unled riders can compete on level terms. Led classes tend to be confined to the youngest age group – eight years and under is the most common.

Unless the schedule states otherwise, assume that the age specified applies to the day of the show. If it is your ninth birthday on the show date, you are not eligible for that group. If, however, the schedule says that the rider must be eight years or under on 1 January, you can have had your ninth birthday at any time since 1 January and still take part in that age group. If you are in any doubt, ring the show secretary before making your entries and get a ruling.

Now, look at the events chosen for the leading-rein riders. There will probably be four or five races, which will take place one after the other. The entry fee for each race will be stated on the schedule and there may be a reduction if you enter them all. Some shows ask for entries to be made on a form and sent to the secretary by a closing date, usually three or four days before the date of the show. More and more shows these days, however, ask for gymkhana entries to be made on the day. If this is the case, do not send your entry in beforehand, even if you are entering other classes at the same show. Just remember to take your entry money with you on the day.

The races selected for leading-rein riders vary from show to show and if you are not sure what is involved, the following descriptions may help.

Ball and Bucket

The leading-rein version of this popular game does not usually require riders to dismount. Each competitor has to collect a number of balls one at a time from the far end of the arena and drop them into a bucket placed near the start line. Rolled-up socks or potatoes may be used instead of tennis balls. If the balls are placed on an upturned bin, the handler should manoeuvre the pony so that the rider can reach out to collect a ball and repeat the manoeuvre at the bucket end to allow the rider to lean down and drop the ball. If the balls have been placed on the ground, the handler usually picks one up and hands it to the rider. Errors, such as a fallen ball or upset bucket, may be corrected by the handler.

Ball and Racquet

A tennis ball has to be balanced on a tennis racquet and carried in and out of a line of bending posts. The ball may not be touched by hand while it is held on the racquet but fallen balls may be picked up and replaced by the handler. This is quite a difficult game for young riders even if they do not have to worry about controlling the pony, and is therefore not often selected for a leading-rein programme.

Bending

One of the most popular races for all age groups. Each rider has to bend up a line of four, five or six poles, round the end one and back again. It does not test the skill of the leading-rein rider at all since all she has to do is to sit tight and hold on. The winner in this case will always be the pony which leads well behind a fast handler. Nevertheless, it is regularly included in a leading-rein section.

Bottle Race

A litre-size lemonade bottle made of plastic and weighted is placed on an upturned bin at the far end of the arena. A similar bottle is given to the rider. The rider places one bottle on a vacant upturned bin on the way up the arena, collects the bottle at the far end and returns to the finish. Here again, this is a difficult race for small children as the bottles are quite cumbersome and hard for very small hands to hold.

Coloured Corners

An extremely popular game for leading-rein riders as everything depends on luck and absolutely no skill or dexterity is required. Four cones mark the corners of an imaginary square and a

Leading-rein Bending. The handler has the pony under control but the rider is able to use her legs to keep the pony moving forward.

different coloured flag is placed in each cone. Riders follow one another round the square to music. When the music stops, each rider goes to a corner and stops. The judge has counters corresponding in colour to the flags and, without looking at the riders, draws a counter and calls out the colour. All riders unlucky enough to be caught at that flag are out and must leave the arena. The game continues until only one rider is left.

Crossing the River

Another game which largely depends on luck. Two jumping poles are placed on the ground about thirty feet (9.1 metres) apart. These represent the banks of a river. Riders follow each other to music across the 'river'. When the music stops, everyone stands still and any pony caught in the 'river' is out.

Dressing-up Race

Riders are led to a point at the far end of the arena where some type of garment is hung on a pole or placed on a bin. The handler gives the garment to the rider who must put it on before setting off for the finish. Hats, mufflers, pyjama jackets etc. are all suitable for use in this race.

Eating and Drinking Race

A 'meal' – usually a biscuit and a plastic cup of water – is placed on a bin or table at the far end of the arena. The rider has to dismount, eat the biscuit and drink the water before remounting and riding to the finish. Handlers may help their charges to remount.

Egg and Spoon Race

This may be played in two ways. In the first, the rider carries a spoon containing an egg (usually hard-boiled!) up and down a line of bending posts without touching the egg with the hand. A fallen egg may be replaced by the handler. In the second, the egg and spoon are placed on the ground at the far end of the arena. The rider dismounts, picks up the spoon containing the egg and without touching the egg runs on foot back to the finish. The competitor may replace the egg if it is dropped. Handlers follow at a safe distance with the ponies.

Flag Race

Riders have to transfer flags from one cone to another in turn. The number of flags used in this race is at the discretion of the organiser but it is essential in any version of this race that the rider is the one who collects the flag from one cone and places it in the other. The handler's job is to manoeuvre the pony so that the rider's task is simplified, although handlers may be allowed to pick up fallen flags and hand them to the rider, or straighten upset cones.

Jelly Baby Gobble

This game is possibly more fun for the spectators than for the competitors. Each rider has to take a jelly baby from a plate of flour, using only their teeth and without touching it with the

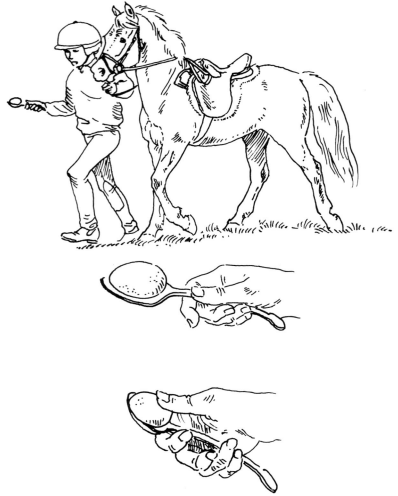

A pony that leads well is vitally important in an Egg and Spoon Race because you can concentrate on keeping the egg in the spoon. Remember that you *must* hold the spoon by its stem (small picture, top) and not steady it with your thumb (bottom).

hand. The position of the plate depends on how far the organisers want the pony to be led: sometimes the plate is at the far end of the arena; sometimes the rider has to go round an end pole or cone and back to the plate. Leading-rein riders are usually allowed a leg-up after they have grabbed the jelly baby, and handlers should take care to keep ponies at a safe distance whilst the riders are dismounted.

Knickerbocker Glory

This race is a means of using the top half of a cone after it has been cut off to make a wider container for the Flag Race. Turned upside down, it forms a cup on which the rider must balance a plastic ball. Riders have to carry the cones up and down lines of bending poles without losing the ball which must, of course, not be touched by the hand. If the ball falls, the handler should be allowed to replace it on the cone.

Mug Race

There are different versions of this game, all of which involve transferring a number of mugs one at a time from one pole to another or from an upturned bin to one or more poles. The shape of the mug often determines the rules of the game as plastic tumblers can be stacked on top of each other while metal beakers with handles must be placed singly on poles. It is quite good for leading-rein riders, testing their dexterity. Handlers are usually allowed to retrieve fallen mugs although the rider has the task of placing them on the poles.

Musical Mats/Poles/Chairs

Musical games have long been popular in gymkhanas and all operate on the same principle: riders move round the perimeter of a circle until the music stops, at which point they ride, or dismount and run, to the mats, poles or chairs in the centre. Someone always ends up without a mat, and is therefore eliminated. Mats and chairs are best for little ones, as the handler may remain on the outside of the circle while the rider runs to the centre and there is no risk of a child being kicked while on the ground. A mat is removed at the end of each round until only one is left which is contested by the only two riders left in the competition. Obviously, this game favours the older leading-rein riders. If possible, ponies should be led round in an anti-clockwise direction (on the left rein) so that riders may dismount on the correct side and do not have to duck behind or in front of the pony when they begin their dash for the centre.

Musical Statues

This game is similar to the above, except that riders do not dismount and do not have to go into the centre. When the music stops, pony, rider and handler all freeze. Anyone who moves is out. The disadvantage of this game is that there are nearly always several ponies which will stand still on command. These few may be so evenly matched that things like a swishing tail, a nod of the head or even a twitching ear may be needed to settle the placings.

Ride and Run

Competitors ride to the far end of the arena, dismount and run to the finish. Handlers follow the riders home at a safe distance.

Sack Race

A line of sacks (preferably hessian ones, although these are hard to come by these days) are laid out on the ground, their openings facing towards the finish. The rider is led up the arena, round a marker and back to the sack. After dismounting, each competitor gets into the sack and jumps or shuffles her way to the finish. Rules for holding the sack up at least to waist height are usually fairly strict. Handlers should keep at a safe distance as they follow the riders home.

Shoe Scramble

Shoes, one for each rider, are hidden in a pile of loose straw at the end of the arena. A matching shoe is handed to the rider when they reach the straw. Handlers hold the ponies while the riders search the straw for their shoe's partner. Once they have made up a pair, riders remount and ride to the finish.

Stepping-Stone Dash

Riders are led up the arena and dismount when they reach the stepping-stones (five or six upturned flowerpots or blocks placed in a line, one set for each competitor). They must negotiate the stepping-stones, remount and continue round a marker and back to the finish. If they fail to negotiate the stepping-stones correctly they must start again with the first one.

Sword Race

Rings are mounted on the top of bending poles, usually three or four to a lane. Riders carry wooden swords and have to collect the rings on the swords while riding up the line. When all the rings have been collected, the riders rush to the finish. This is a fast and furious game when played by older riders and the leading-rein version is rather more sedate, but it is a good one for testing the skill of the rider.

Tyre Race

Another race played up and down the arena. A lightweight motorcycle tyre is placed on the ground halfway up the arena. Each rider has to dismount, get through the tyre, remount and ride to the finish. Handlers may help riders on and off the ponies.

Walk and Trot

This is popular with organisers because it does not require any equipment but it is difficult to judge and boring for competitors. Nevertheless, it is often included in a leading-rein section. Riders have to walk up the arena and trot back. If the pony breaks into a faster pace than the one he is supposed to be doing, the competitor must turn a circle before continuing. The main difficulty for the judge lies in watching all the contestants at the same time. It is also hard for the handler, who is running ahead of the pony, to realise that the pony has increased his pace, even for a stride or two.

A young rider tackles the Sword Race in a calm way. The pony, who seems equally laid-back, is probably an old hand, prepared to carry out the games at whatever speed his rider chooses.

It is clear from the above list that show organisers have quite a variety of games to choose from. Some organisers come up with their own inventions and many games can be quite ingenious.

If you do not know the race listed in the schedule, never be put off entering. The rules for each race will always be explained at the start and, even then, if you are not quite clear you are perfectly entitled to ask any questions.

Remember that the people who act as gymkhana judges have usually had children themselves and know just what it is like to be an inexperienced competitor. You will find them sympathetic and generally very patient.

Chapter Two
How To Help Your Pony

No one ever forgets their first pony. If you are lucky your memories will all be happy ones: the fun you had, the rides you went on, the gymkhanas you enjoyed. A good, long-suffering first pony is the best introduction to riding anyone can have.

First ponies need to be long-suffering. A young rider's seat in the saddle is very precarious and can easily be upset by an unexpected movement, and it is natural for a novice rider who feels insecure to jerk the reins, grab the mane or clutch the pommel.

First ponies are also very experienced. This can work two ways; an experienced pony has seen it all. We do not know how long a memory an animal has, but a pony that has been ill-treated or badly frightened in the past will show signs of fear if he finds himself in what he perceives to be similar circum-stances. Many ponies, for example, are nervous of men or of noisy things like tractors or motorbikes. And a pony that has suffered, say, an accident on the road is likely to be traffic-shy for the rest of his life. These are negative memories.

A lifetime of gentle handling, however, generates positive reactions. A good first pony takes care of his young rider, somehow sensing his rider's reactions and adjusting his pace accordingly. Such a pony stands patiently while inexpert, small hands struggle to pick out his feet. He submits to being thumped with a dandy brush while his young owner grooms him and never minds having his mane and tail 'smartened up'. He lowers his head obligingly when being bridled, opens his mouth when the bit bangs against his teeth and waits without moving while buckles are fumblingly fastened. He accepts the saddle without protest even if the hair on his back has been ruffled the wrong way, and he *never* blows out his belly when his girth is being done up.

On a ride, this paragon goes where his rider wants him to go, even without being asked, moves faster when his saddle flap is kicked and slows down when the reins are tugged. As for snatching mouthfuls of grass or moving swiftly to the nearest patch of grass and refusing to leave it, well, such a thought would never cross his mind.

Of course, ponies are not paragons. The best you can hope for from your first pony is that he will at least have some of the virtues listed above.

Small children love their ponies. Given half a chance, they would take them to bed with them and, since that is not possible, they spend much of the time hugging and kissing their furry friend.

But ponies are flesh and blood, and it is very important that young children learn to appreciate the fact. Even when a child is very small, it is not too soon to ensure that owning a pony is recognised as a responsibility. Until a rider is eight or nine years old – or later still, depending on the child – handling and riding a pony should never be carried out without adult supervision. Nevertheless, while the grown-up might be there in the background, the child should be encouraged to do most of the work herself.

Catching the pony

A small child should be capable of entering a field, offering a titbit to the pony, putting on a headcollar and leading the pony to the gate. Always accompany a child in this task and ensure that any other ponies in the field will not interfere. If the other ponies are at all pushy, a small child should not be allowed to catch her own pony for fear of coming to harm: flying heels are just at head height for a young child. But if the pony lives alone or the adult can catch and hold any other ponies in the field, the child will gain a sense of achievement by catching her own pony. She will also learn important lessons in the art of catching ponies, such as approaching from the front and slightly to one side, standing still when a few feet from the pony and allowing him to approach, holding the titbit on an outstretched palm and slipping the rope of the headcollar round the neck of the pony before putting the headcollar in place.

The child also learns how to lead the pony and to hold the leadrope. She needs to be told not to wrap the rope round her hand but to hold the rope a few inches from the ring with her right hand and the other end of the rope with her left. Before long she will know that a pony follows more obediently if the handler walks alongside the pony's head or just in front, and that no self-respecting pony will take being hauled about or tugged along by someone who stares him in the eye and pulls.

Grooming a pony

This is not an easy task however well-behaved the pony. It requires strength as well as dedication, especially if, as is likely, he lives in a field and gets muddy. Little children quickly get bored or spend the time grooming the same spot over and over again. The best plan is for the adult to help with the grooming, concentrating on the difficult bits – the legs, under the belly and dock, around the head – and let the child deal with the neck and body. A stiff-bristled dandy brush is not a good brush for a child to use; a body brush is better as the softer bristles can do less harm.

Picking out the feet must be done properly but small children find it difficult to support the foot and wield a hoof pick at the same time. If an adult picks up each foot in turn and points out the different parts of the foot, showing the tender bits and how to handle a hoof pick correctly, the child will learn lessons that will benefit her in the future.

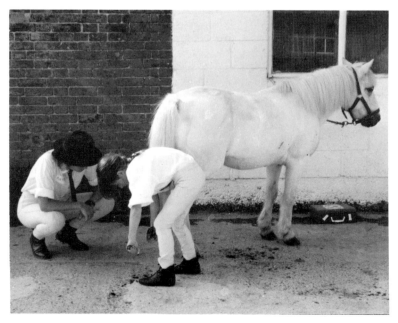

Under supervision, small children can learn the proper care of a pony – like this young rider busily picking out her pony's foot.

25

Tying up

All ponies need to be tied up from time to time and it never hurts to teach a child at an early age the correct – and safest – way to do so. A quick-release knot is one of the simplest to tie but is more difficult for small hands if the leadrope is new or stiff. For a first pony, therefore, equip the halter with a well-used, flexible, soft rope and encourage the child to practise tying the knot away from the pony. All rings for tying up should have a loop of string or baler twine to which the rope may be fastened. This provides a safety back-up in an emergency should the quick-release knot fail to fulfil its purpose as the string will break or can quickly be cut.

Tacking up

If the pony is small enough, young riders should be taught the proper way to put on a saddle and bridle as early as possible. This may mean waiting until a child is tall enough to be able to place the saddle on the pony's back, and most small children will need help. Nevertheless, all children can learn the importance of putting the saddle gently on the withers and pushing it back into the correct position so that the hairs underneath lie the right way. Even when a grown-up has to carry out this part of the operation, the child can help by going round to the offside, checking that the saddle flap has not been tucked up and that the girth is not twisted, and passing the girth under the belly to the adult on the nearside. Fastening the girth is best done by the helper – few small children have sufficient strength to draw the girth tight, but they can certainly be aware of the importance of a well-fastened girth and learn to check the girth before setting off on a ride.

Bridling is difficult unless the pony is particularly co-operative. A pony soon learns that simply by raising his head he can put himself out of reach of a small child. Nevertheless, the child can be taught to hold a bridle by the headpiece in her left hand and to put the reins over the pony's head with her right. Balancing the bit on the palm of the left hand and offering it to the pony whilst keeping tension on the bridle with the right hand can also be learned. The child can be shown how to encourage a pony to open his mouth by inserting the thumb into the corner of the mouth. If necessary,

An earnest discussion – young children learning how to behave when close to a pony, advised here by an older rider.

pictures may be used to help describe the shape of the mouth and to indicate the position of the pony's teeth.

General care

No child old enough to ride is too young to learn about caring for a pony. The fact that a pony is a living creature, that he must be fed and watered at regular intervals, and that he must always be treated with kindness and consideration are all vital lessons. A small child can fill haynets and buckets, even if someone older has to carry them to the pony. She can look to the pony's comfort before worrying about her own and learn to offer water before a feed or not to ride too soon after feeding.

An early apprenticeship in ponycare will prepare young riders for a lifetime with horses.

Chapter Three
How To Help Yourself

If you want to be good at gymkhana games, you do not only need a good pony. Many games call for manual dexterity and this is something that even quite small children can practise at home.

In most leading-rein classes, it is quite apparent that the young competitors have never had any practice at all. They fumble when placing a mug on a pole, they have no idea how to put a flag in a cone or drop a sock into a bucket, they fall over when asked to run a few yards in a sack. Yet all these tasks are not difficult in themselves, and since these novice riders do not have to worry about controlling their ponies, there is no reason why they should not become very good at handling gymkhana equipment.

A good way to prepare yourself for gymkhanas to come is to set up equipment on the lawn and do everything you would do at a normal gymkhana, but without your ponies.

Older children can be a great help here because they can show little ones just how it is done. To make it more fun you could even organise your own – dismounted – gymkhana and invite all your friends.

If you do not have much room or not enough equipment, organise the races as team events, with as many competitors in each team as you like. The best events to choose for these fun afternoons would be Ball or Sock and Bucket, Bottle Race, Egg and Spoon Race, Flag Race, Mug Race, Sack Race and Tyre Race. The rules for all these events can be found in Part IV (page 97). Just forget about the ponies. A garden cane can be used instead of a bending pole in the Mug Race, and remember not to use too long a cane or small children will not be able to reach up and put a mug on it.

Everyone will enjoy themselves. Better still, they will learn to handle equipment properly, which will stand them in good stead when a proper gymkhana comes along.

While young riders are learning gymkhana techniques, they can also be taught about the best sort of clothing to wear for mounted games. Some show schedules do not mention dress in their rules, and they may not mention saddlery either.

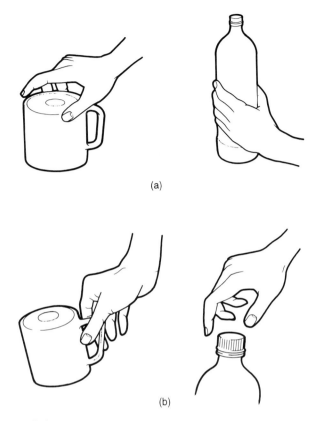

(a)

(b)

Pony Club rules, however, are very strict. Even if you are still at the leading-rein stage, it is a good idea to know what you and your pony should wear at a gymkhana.

Rider's clothing

Hat
This should conform to the highest safety standards. These standards do get updated from time to time as manufacturing techniques and materials improve, but the British Standard kite-mark is a good indication. Lightweight crash caps are now widely available and are comfortable to wear, even for very small children. They should be supplied with a chinstrap, properly anchored at at least three points. All children should learn at a very early age never

to sit on a pony without wearing a proper hat, with the chinstrap fastened. Provided this rule is enforced at all times, it soon becomes second nature to put on a hat before getting on a horse.

In the Pony Club, only black or navy covers are allowed for hats. Ordinary gymkhana organisers do not object to coloured ones.

Boots

Jodhpur boots are made in very small sizes and even the tiniest child should be able to find a pair that will fit. Jodhpur boots, rather than long boots, are best for gymkhanas as it is easier to run in them. The important features of jodhpur boots are the heel and the continuous sole. The heel prevents the foot from slipping right through the stirrup iron; a half sole could catch on the iron and trap the foot – dangerous if the rider falls off. Trainers, wellington boots and flat pumps are unsafe for riding, the first two because they are wide and have ridged soles, both of which could trap the foot in the iron, the pumps because they have no heel. The Pony Club will not allow muckers for competitions.

Jodhpurs

Jodhpurs are reinforced inside the knee to prevent chafing. Because they are usually made of stretch material, they are comfortable and allow freedom of movement. Jeans are not allowed at most gymkhanas although an exception might be made for leading-rein riders. They are, however, not recommended for riding because they can chafe. Chaps – leather leg protectors – are worn with jeans to prevent chafing, but they are not considered suitable for organised games.

Jackets

Jackets are worn for showing and jumping and they are not forbidden for gymkhanas. They are, however, quite restricting for the sort of activity mounted games require.

Sweatshirts and jerseys

These are ideal for gymkhanas as they are tidy, comfortable and provide protection for the arms.

Shirts

On hot days, short-sleeved shirts are acceptable at most gymkhanas, although some organisers may insist on a long-sleeved shirt or sweatshirt. T-shirts are generally considered rather untidy. In

Pony Club team competitions, the rule is that long-sleeved white shirts should be worn, with white jerseys permissible on cold days. Pony Club teams wear tabards over their shirts in the team colours.

Ties
These are not necessary for gymkhanas.

Whips and spurs
These are *never* allowed in any gymkhana competition.

Saddlery

Bridles
An ordinary leather bridle with a snaffle bit is stipulated by the Pony Club. Other gymkhana organisers may not be so fussy and will permit such bits as Pelhams or Kimblewicks. Few gymkhana organisers, however, will allow the use of a bitless bridle or a snaffle with a twisted mouthpiece.

Cavessons and various kinds of drop nosebands are allowed, and both standing and running martingales can be used.

Saddles
In Pony Club competitions, only general purpose leather saddles are permitted. At other gymkhanas, pad saddles, with or without a half-tree, may be allowed. The stirrup bars on the saddles should be fitted with safety catches and the girths should have two buckles.

Bandages and boots
Support bandages, brushing boots and overreach boots may be worn by the pony.

Studs
Fitted to the hind shoes, studs are allowed in Pony Club competitions. They should not be necessary in leading-rein classes.

Tack inspection
This is a very important feature of Pony Club competitions. Every pony taking part is rigorously inspected before the games begin, not merely to see that the tack conforms to the rules but also to check its condition. Woe betide any rider whose stirrup

leathers, bridle parts or girths have any frayed or broken stitching. Bent or worn buckles or poorly stuffed saddles could also cause the offender to be sent off to find replacements. At ordinary gymkhanas, there is no official tack inspection, but the judge or collecting ring steward could still refuse to allow a pony with tack in a dangerous condition to take part.

Part 2

The Middle Years

Chapter One
Joining a Pony Club Squad

All young riders will benefit from joining the Pony Club. For those who want to be good at gymkhanas, membership is essential because it is in the Pony Club that you will get the best training from very experienced adults as well as help from older members who not so long ago were in the same position as yourself.

The Pony Club is now a worldwide organisation. In English-speaking countries, it has been established for many years, but the movement is now beginning to spread through Europe. It was formed in Britain in 1929 and there are more than 350 branches in the UK alone. In Australia there are even more members than there are in Britain, while in New Zealand, the USA, Canada and Eire membership can be measured in thousands. In Europe, it is most popular in the Netherlands where several thousand young riders belong to more than 150 branches.

If you live in Britain, you will almost certainly have a branch in your neighbourhood. Pony Club Headquarters at the British Equestrian Centre, Stoneleigh, Warwickshire (the full address is given at the end of the book) can put you in touch with the secretary of your nearest branch. Once you have paid your entrance fee and annual subscription, you will be eligible to join in any of the activities organised by your branch. Most of these activities take place in the holidays and include fun events as well as what are known as working rallies.

A working rally is a gathering of members at which instruction is given free; this may be instruction in flatwork and jumping, in grooming and feeding, or on such important topics as the care of a pony's feet or keeping your pony healthy. Rallies may be mounted or dismounted. Fun events include scavenger and treasure hunts, barbecues, discos, gymkhana afternoons and picnics.

The Pony Club also organises interbranch competitions, some of which are qualifiers for the annual championships. The major championships are horse trials, show jumping, polo, polocrosse, dressage, tetrathlon and mounted games. The last named, for which the principal trophy is the Prince Philip Cup awarded at the finals at the Horse of the Year Show in October every year, is responsible for the enormous increase in gymkhana skills over the last few years.

When you take part in an ordinary gymkhana, you will almost certainly realise that there are one or two competitors who are quite outstanding. If you are not very good yourself, you will no doubt try to avoid competing in the same heat as one of the stars. Some people even complain that these excellent performers should not be allowed to take part in run-of-the-mill gymkhanas, arguing that it is not fair to the other competitors. This seems to be a very negative way of looking at things, for it means that you have little incentive to improve your own gymkhana skills.

While there are bound to be differences in ability – some children are naturally more athletic than others, and some ponies are faster and easier to control – the quickest way to get better at gymkhana events is to join the mounted games squad of your local Pony Club branch.

Most trainers will accept children into the squad at the age of seven or eight. At this age, a young rider can look forward to taking part in Pony Club mounted games for the next seven years or so. A member of the Pony Club games team must not have reached his or her fifteenth birthday by 1 January in any year. For a junior games team, the age limit is twelve.

The younger you start training, therefore, the better.

In most branches, regular practices are organised on a weekly basis and, if an indoor school is available, will be held through-out the winter or start as soon as Christmas is over. As area competitions take place out of doors in April and May, practising will move outside as soon as the weather allows, and it reaches a climax as the area competition approaches. Regular interbranch friendly competitions ensure that squad members get some experience in playing the games in competi-tion conditions.

Trainers learn what games are to be used in area and zone competitions (the semi-finals) during the winter, and rules for the current season are sent to the branches in late January or early February. The games are chosen by the Pony Club's Mounted Games Committee and are designed to test a variety of skills, some games depending on speed, others on precision and care. Only one race – Bending – figures in the programme every year, but the more popular races – such as Sock and Bucket – crop up regularly. At least one race will call for two members of each team to compete together.

Although gymkhana skills are important whether you are riding as an individual or as part of a team, team games have an added dimension. In the first place, a team member will carry out the necessary task only once; in the second, riders have to hand over items of equipment to the next rider to go, so that the hand-over becomes a vital factor in the team's ability to win.

Once a trainer knows what games are scheduled for the year, he or she will gather together the equipment necessary for practising. Some of the richer branches buy all the appropriate equipment from the Pony Club's recognised supplier (see addresses in Appendix), often buying sufficient to run a complete competition. Other trainers have to make do. Nevertheless, whatever branch you belong to, you can be assured that your trainer will have whatever is needed even if he or she has to scrounge, borrow or improvise.

In the early days of training, your instructor will no doubt concentrate on teaching you to handle your pony in a games situation. At first, you may not be given much opportunity to test your skills against another member of the squad. If the training sessions are held in an indoor school, they may feel very like an instructional rally as you follow other members of the squad around the arena. The difference is that you will be learning techniques that are important in carrying out the games successfully.

You will almost certainly find it quite difficult at first as you have to concentrate on controlling your pony with one hand while handling equipment with the other. Experienced riders make it look so easy and it is tempting to assume that this is because they have perfectly trained ponies. It can be quite a revelation – and, indeed, something of a shock – when your trainer suggests that members of the squad swap ponies. Suddenly, your badly behaved pony becomes a model of co-operation when ridden by a knowledgeable games player. And whatever happened to that brilliant little pony with his twinkling feet and perfectly executed turns now you are sitting on his back?

The truth is that the ability to play gymkhana games successfully is not something that happens by chance. Of course, it helps if you are naturally athletic and it helps, too, if you have a pony which enjoys gymkhanas, but getting your act together properly, reliably and confidently comes about through a combination of hard work and dedication. If you are a member of a games team, you have four colleagues who are depending on you to get things right. As an individual competitor, if you make a mistake, the only person you are letting down is yourself.

When you watch a really good Pony Club games team in action, you will be impressed at how easy they manage to make each manoeuvre appear. Even if a mistake does happen, no time is wasted on recriminations; the culprit corrects the mistake in a flash and continues the game without further ado, often so well that any time lost is quickly made up. Other members of the team shout encouragement; nobody blames anybody else. A good team develops a tremendous spirit of co-operation and support, helping the trainer to get the best out of each rider and encouraging every member to overcome weaknesses.

Chapter Two
Training Your Pony

Anyone, whether human or equine, can easily get bored if asked to do the same thing over and over again. In training your pony to become a first-class games player, it is important to remember this.

You may well have been told that ponies are best taught by repetition, and this certainly forms the basis of a training programme, but repetition must be tempered by common sense. There is no point in spending all afternoon bending up and down a row of poles, but ten or fiteen minutes a day, followed by a relaxed ride, will keep your pony interested.

When you acquire a pony suitable for gymkhanas, first find out from his previous owners exactly what sort of experience he has had. Clearly, if he has been part of a Pony Club games squad for a number of years, he may well end up training you; but not every child enters gymkhanas and your new pony could still be quite a novice.

Fortunately for those who seek to do well in gymkhana competitions, equipment for practising with is quite easy to acquire. It is not as though you or your parents have to buy a full set of coloured show jumps, which could be necessary if show jumping is your forte. Nor do you have to go to the expense of building a number of cross-country jumps.

Everyone has buckets; there are probably a few bamboo canes which can be borrowed from the garden shed; most households have a tennis ball or two. Squash bottles and washing-up liquid containers can be retrieved from the dustbin, and empty ice-cream boxes are not hard to find. If your mother objects to your borrowing her rubbish bin, a kitchen chair will double up as a table. Save old socks which are worn out or have lost their partners. The only things you will have to buy are a few cones.

If possible, arrange practice sessions with a friend. It is more fun for everyone and you can help each other to improve.

Start practising in the spring, as soon as the evenings are light enough for you to get in half-an-hour or so after school and

Ask your friends to help you get your pony accustomed to all sorts of noises and other hazards. Here, a pony learns that clanking buckets are no threat. The more he is exposed to flapping sacks, waving canes and flags and bouncing balls, the more indifferent to them he will become.

before you have to settle down to homework. If possible, take a radio or cassette-player into the field with you to get your pony used to unusual sounds.

If your pony seems nervous of some pieces of equipment, take things slowly. Many ponies are nervous of flags until they learn that there is nothing to worry about. The best way of doing this is to make four flags (see page 131) out of the most colourful material you can find and place them in a cone in a prominent position. Let your pony have a look at them – he may snort at first but he will be curious. Talk to him soothingly, and then take him away from the flags and ignore them for the rest of the day. Be very patient. If you repeat the process – the quiet approach, the soothing talk and then taking no further notice of the flags – every day for a week, the pony will soon accept the flags as part of the scenery.

The next stage is to get your pony used to your having a flag in your hand. Dismount and walk quietly up to the cone, leading the pony. Take a flag with your spare hand. The pony may have become so used to the flags that he is quite unconcerned and you will know that it was unfamiliarity rather than fear that made him nervous in the first place. If, however, he jumps back and shows every sign of panicking, simply put the flag on the ground, calm the pony down and walk him away. Leave it till the next day before trying again.

It is this very slow, gentle approach to the problem which will eventually bring success. Even if it takes you three or four weeks, your pony will eventually realise that flags hold no terrors and you will be able to ride him up to the cone, remove a flag, wave it round your head and replace it in the cone.

The same process should be used with any other pieces of equipment.

Starting, stopping and standing still – these are all vital factors in gymkhana success. How often have you watched an event in which a race is lost because the pony runs backwards at the start, or will not stop at a bucket, or having stopped will not stand still?

It is not always the pony's fault. A carefully schooled pony has been taught to move up and down the paces gradually. He walks, trots and canters obediently. He comes to a halt when given the correct aids. He stands still until told to move off.

Unfortunately, apart from the latter instruction, mounted games call for a quite different approach. The pony must stand still at the start but, like a coiled spring, leap into a gallop as soon as the signal is given. He must learn to stop from a gallop. These movements are certainly not part of a normal dressage test.

Teach him slowly. Start by making him stand still while you count to ten, then urge him into a trot. Do this a few times, then try going straight into a canter. The aids are no different from those you have been taught – it is just the speed of transition which is different.

A similar process is used in stopping. Trot to the end of the practice area, use your legs to push your pony on to the bit, flex your wrists and pull gently on the bit. When the pony stops, relax your hands and give the pony plenty of praise. Keep practising the movement at increasing speeds until your pony is sliding to a halt from a gallop.

Use your voice at all times. Ponies respond to the human voice although many young riders tend to forget this. It is a most important aid.

41

Teaching your pony to lead willingly is also valuable. Remember that ponies do not like to be looked at when they are being led. If your pony is a reluctant leader, encourage him with a few titbits and walk confidently ahead of him. He will soon follow you happily. Gradually increase the speed, so that the pony has to trot to keep up with you. After a while, your pony will even be prepared to canter beside you.

The various manoeuvres do not have to be practised only in a school or a field. Whenever you are out on a ride, you can occasionally ask for a flying start or a rapid halt. You can practise riding with one hand – this involves neck-reining which is described in the next chapter. You can dismount and remount and train your pony to lead.

Ponies ridden by members of a games team have one other problem to face which does not affect the individual games player. This is the change-over between one rider in a team and another, a moment when many games are won or lost.

In a team game, each rider performs whatever skill the game requires and then returns to the start to hand over an item of equipment. The pony waiting on the start line has to face another pony galloping towards him, while his own rider is leaning forward, one hand on the reins, the other outstretched, shouting encouragement to her team-mate.

The rules are very strict. The hand-over must take place behind the start line. Woe betide the over-eager pony which sets just one foot into the playing arena before his rider has the baton, ball, bottle or flag safely in her hand. The incoming rider, jubilant at having successfully completed her share of the game and anxious to waste as little time as possible, rides homeward as fast as she can.

Any self-respecting pony in this situation is likely to back away from the other. He may jump sideways to avoid a collision. In either case, his actions make the hand-over even more difficult than it already is.

Practice is needed to teach the ponies to trust their riders and to understand that there will be sufficient space between them to prevent a collision, that there is no need to run backwards or dance to the side.

As with any other type of training, start slowly and gradually increase the pace of the approach. Obviously, you need a friend to help, preferably one who is also in the games squad. Take it in turns to be the rider on the start line. Ensure that the incoming

Ponies that lead well are important. What you need is a pony like the top one which trots happily at his owner's side. The bottom pony will get even more stubborn if his rider turns to look at him as she tries to drag him along.

rider approaches your pony at a walk, then build up to a trot and finish at a canter.

Sometimes a third friend, especially one with a nice, calm, solid pony, can help. If your pony jumps sideways, practise the hand-over with the calm pony standing alongside him. Not only will your pony gain confidence from the other pony's calmness, he will physically be unable to move sideways without barging into his companion. Of course, you cannot have the third rider beside you in a competition but if you have practised enough at home your pony should have learned to stand still.

Ponies which back off can be encouraged not to do so by walking them forwards as the incoming pony arrives at the start. It will mean standing further back than you would normally expect to do and you have to learn to judge the moment when you begin to move forwards, but a moving pony will find it difficult to change direction.

If, however, you have a pony which is brilliant at the games but cannot be trained to stand quietly in the face of an incoming pony, there is only one solution. You will always have to go first in the team. That way, your pony will always be the incoming one during a change-over and, for some reason, possibly because the other pony is standing still, this rarely presents any problems.

Chapter Three
Learning Difficult Manoeuvres

If you get the chance, spare a moment to study a really good Pony Club games team in action. Although they may occasionally make mistakes, most of the time their performance is relaxed, fluid and fast. They pick up items in one quick, decisive movement, they place things in containers sharply and confidently. They hand over or receive objects without hesitating and, usually, without dropping them. In a game like Ball and Bucket, they can bend so close to the bucket that their hands are below the rim of the bucket when the ball is released. Even on the rare occasions when an item is dropped accidentally, they can pick it up without getting off. Most telling of all, they mount and dismount without checking their ponies.

Yet, hard though it may be to believe, they were not born with these skills. Their successes are due to hard work, regular practising and, probably, some athletic training. You, too, could join their ranks.

Vaulting

This is the name given to the act of leaping astride a pony while he is moving. It looks easy when done well, and any rider can learn the technique. In essence, there are two important elements: the pony must be moving and the rider must get her timing right.

To understand exactly what happens, you should analyse the process. When you understand it, go out into a field with your pony and try it. Although you may fail the first few times, keep trying, because when you have managed it once it will then become easier to get the vault every time.

The reason the pony has to be moving is because you have to use the forward motion to swing yourself into the saddle. Start by urging your pony into a trot and then run along beside him with your left hand on the rein and your right arm over the

Practising the vault. On the left the rider jumps, both feet together. On the right she is almost in position, with the pony's forward movement carrying her into the saddle.

pommel of the saddle, grasping the front flap on the far side with your right hand. Watch your pony's front legs. When the nearside hoof hits the ground, jump with both feet together and spring upwards, taking your weight on your right arm and swinging your right leg over the saddle. If you can manage this correctly and in one fluid movement, you have achieved a successful vault. Practise every day until you are confident that you can get into the saddle every time. Then practise the same movement from the opposite side. A good games player should be able to get on her pony quickly and easily from either side.

The value of the vault cannot be doubted. How often have you seen a rider at a gymkhana event hopping around with one foot in the stirrup and the other on the ground, trying to get on a lively pony which is anxious to be off? By the time she is in position, the rider who can vault has already passed the winning post. Remember that in most games where having to remount is part of the rules, the judge does not mind where you get on as long as you are astride the pony as you cross the finishing line. The vault also saves time if you have to dismount to pick up dropped equipment.

Placing a flag in a cone. The rider guides the pony closely round the cone, neck-reining with her left hand while she concentrates on inserting the flag with her right.

Neck-reining

This is a riding technique typical of Western riders, whose horses are guided by the pressure of the reins on their necks. The ability to apply the technique to a gymkhana pony is vital in any game where you are required to carry an item of equipment, especially if in the process you have to bend in and out of the poles.

To teach your pony to respond to the neck rein, start by using both hands and exaggerate the normal method of steering. If you wish to turn to the right, carry your right hand outwards, feeling the bit on that side, and take your left hand across his withers to ensure that there is pressure from the left rein on his neck. Reverse the movement when turning to the left. At first, you have to exaggerate the signals because the pony will start by responding to pressure on the bit. That, after all, is what he has been taught. Gradually, however, you will find that pressure on the directional rein can be reduced and the pony will learn to move away from the neck rein. Once he is doing that successfully, you will be able to

47

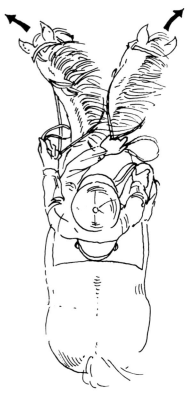

Neck-reining is vital to success in mounted games. This diagram shows the movement in an exaggerated fashion. As your pony learns what is expected of him, a simple turn of the wrist is all that will be needed to make him change direction.

reduce the movement until, simply by turning the hand that holds the reins from one side to another, you can guide the pony in any direction. Always keep the signal as gentle as you can and avoid jerking the reins which will give the pony the opposite instructions. The palm of your hand should be held downwards and your wrist should be supple and flexed.

Do not forget the leg aids when neck-reining. They should be applied first before turning your wrist slightly. It helps, too, if you hold your hands higher than you normally would.

Dismounting

Everything to do with gymkhana games is about saving time. If you wait till your pony has stopped before dismounting you will waste valuable seconds. So you need to get off while he is slowing down.

Essentially, you dismount in the usual way but you must land facing forwards and you must start running as soon as your feet touch the ground. There is no time saved if you fall flat on your face. Remember to take your feet out of the stirrups, transfer the reins to your right hand, place your left hand on the pony's neck, your right hand on the pommel and swing your right leg over the pony's back. As you run beside the pony, slide your hand along the rein until you are holding it about six inches (fifteen centimetres) from the bit.

As with vaulting, practise dismounting on both sides.

Handling equipment

Balls
Where a ball has to be removed from the top of a cone, it is very easy to knock it off. In the Ball and Cone Race, it is essential to slow right down as you pick up the ball and grasp it from the top. You then have it ready to park on the next cone. In the Ball and Bucket Race, practise leaning right down your pony's shoulder so that your hand when you release the ball is as close to the rim of the bucket as possible. Never try throwing the ball into the bucket: you will either miss it altogether or it will bounce out.

Batons
These are only used in team games. During the hand-over, the incoming rider should try to hold it vertically. If she points it at the outgoing rider (easy to do in the heat of the moment), it is more difficult to grasp and can easily be dropped.

Bottles
Hold the top of the bottle when placing it on the bin, grasp the neck when picking it up. In a team game, hold it lower down when handing it over so that the outgoing rider has no alternative but to take it at the top and, therefore, in the best position for putting it on the bin.

Dropping the ball into the bucket. By bending so low, the rider ensures that the ball will stay in the bucket even though the pony is moving fast.

Ball and Bucket again. The rider controls the ball by reversing her hand, thus preventing it from falling too far forward and missing the bucket.

Some idea of the speed at which the Flag Race is run when performed by experienced players. This boy wastes no time on the turn and has perfect control of the flag by holding it halfway down the cane.

Flags

The easiest way to insert a flag into a cone is to hold the flag in the palm with the back of the hand upwards. Grip it about halfway along the cane because this will give you the greatest control over the tip. Some novices try holding the cone at the flag end and dropping it into the cone. The problem with this method is that the tip swings, and getting it into the cone at the first attempt becomes a matter of luck.

When plucking a flag from a cone, lean down as you approach the cone, grasp the cane with the palm of your hand facing forwards and lift it sharply upwards, flicking it backwards as soon as it is clear of the cone. The reason for the last movement is that it is only too easy to drag the flag from the cone, knocking the cone over as you do so.

In team games, remember to carry the flag vertically, especially when you are holding it out for the next rider to take. If you carry it like a lance, accidents can happen. Your team trainer will teach you how best to hand it over. Some trainers suggest that you should turn your wrist over so that the flag part of the cane is at the bottom. This enables the outgoing rider to grasp the flag in exactly the best position to place it in the cone and means that she does not have to adjust her grip as she gallops up the arena.

Litter

Lots of riders dread the Litter Race, having nightmares of chasing a piece of litter round the arena, trying to hook it on to end of the cane. It is actually much easier than you think. You must lean down the side of your pony as far as you can so that the cane is not at a very acute angle. If the cane is too upright, you will merely flick the litter further away. Insert the end of the cane into the open end of the litter and use the forward momentum of your pony to get the litter right on to the cane. Bring the cane up sharply into an upright position and the litter should be secure.

Racquets

These are some of the most difficult items of equipment to control successfully. There is a tendency to tip up the head of the racquet in an exaggerated bid to stop the tennis ball from rolling off the end. In fact, provided your pony is moving forwards at a steady pace, the ball will stay in place more readily if you let the head drop a little. It is not a bad idea to practise this action without your pony. Run round the garden with the racquet in your hand and see what the ball does; watch and remember what action you have to take to

Picking up litter. See how the rider holds the cane very short in order to have control as she hooks the litter on to the end.

The Ball and Racquet Race requires immense concentration. Short reins enable the rider to keep her pony on course while she watches the racquet.

avoid dropping the ball. When you transfer the process to the pony's back and, as long as you have practised your neck-reining, you should find it a lot easier than you had feared. As far as possible always keep your eye on the ball. In team games, the ball is often dropped during a change-over. To hand over successfully, the incoming rider should hold the racquet as near to the end as possible, leaving room for her team-mate to grip the handle behind the crosspiece. Assuming that both riders are right-handed, the hand-over should take place when both riders are more or less parallel, offside to offside. The incoming rider holds out the racquet at arm's length, giving room for the other rider to take it from her.

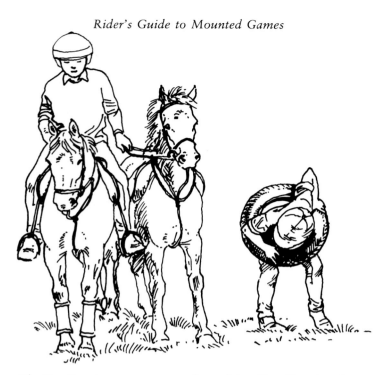

The Tyre Race is a team event or at least a joint effort. Here the rider struggles through the tyre while her pony is held by her team-mate.

Socks

Rolled-up socks are easier to grip and less likely to bounce out when placed in a bucket. In Pony Club team competitions, you are not allowed to put the sock in your mouth as you remount and ride to the bucket. This is a rule which was introduced for hygienic reasons. Other gymkhana organisers may not be so fussy but always check if the rule is operating. There is no point in being disqualified for something which can so easily be avoided.

Tyres

There are two schools of thought as to the best method of getting through a tyre. Some riders favour picking the tyre up, putting it over your head and letting it drop to the ground. Others believe you should step into the tyre and lift it up your body. You should choose the method you feel most comfortable with.

Jockeymanship

Jockeymanship can best be described as the art of being in the right place at the right time. Luck is not involved. Good jockeymanship comes from the skill and knowledge of the rider.

In any game which requires you to collect an item of equipment or to place something accurately, a successful outcome depends on your approach. Most Pony Club team members come up to the cone or bin at an oblique angle. This means that they gallop towards it, slow up when within a few metres of it, move outwards slightly (usually to the left if they are right-handed) and approach the cone at a slant. The reason for this is that the changes of direction inhibit the pony's blind dash, while the oblique approach enables the rider to turn quickly and retrieve her mistake if she misses or drops the ball or bottle.

Principal exceptions to this angled attack are in the Flag Race, where any well-trained rider should be able to collect a flag without checking her pace, and the Sword Race, where maintaining a straight line is important when collecting the rings on

An angled approach in the Pyramid Race. The rider concentrates on placing the carton smoothly on the table.

Diagram showing the best line to take in a Bending Race. Note the wide circle as you reach the last pole, thus ensuring that, when you turn, the line homewards is as straight as possible.

the sword. Experienced riders can get a ball into a bucket without deviating from the line, but novices should stick to the slanted approach.

In bending races, time can be saved by making a good turn round the end pole. As you approach the last pole, move out before you make the turn so that you have a straighter run for the return journey.

Collecting rings from a gallows or hanging letters on hooks always seem to cause problems. This is usually because the rider tackles the task head-on. She rides straight up to the gallows, leans forward and and tries to manipulate the equipment from between her pony's ears. Small wonder that the pony backs off, making the rider's task even more difficult. The right way is to approach the gallows on the right-hand side and then turn across the gallows so that you are parallel with them. You can now use your right hand to collect the ring or hang the letter without worrying your pony.

Most novice riders in gymkhanas keep their reins at the length used for normal riding. This inevitably means that as soon as a rider has a piece of equipment to carry her reins get in an awful tangle as she drops one side altogether and tries to control her pony with flapping reins. Look at the experts. All of them tie a knot in their reins so that they can maintain contact without raising their hands to head-level or getting the loop caught up in their feet.

The knot should lie just in front of the withers. Remember to undo the knot as soon as the gymkhana events are over so that the reins are not damaged in any way.

In all races where you have to dismount, always slip your feet from your stirrups before you start slowing down. Novice riders stop first. In musical races, where you have to avoid

Two competitors in the Pony Club Race. The one on the left is left-handed and has approached the gallows so that her left hand is close to the hooks. The other rider, however, has made her task more difficult by having to reach across her pony. She would have found it easier had she made her approach from the right.

being the odd one out, try to keep some space between you and other competitors. So many riders bunch up and then find that they and everyone near them are all racing for the same mat or pole. Ride alone and there is probably an empty mat near to you which nobody else is going for. In some shows, there may be jumps defining the perimeter of the circle. You cannot control the moment when the music stops and you may well be caught behind a jump before you can ride or run into the centre, but you can minimise the risk by speeding up as you pass the jump and slowing down while you are in the open.

Many races have to be run in heats and this can cause a great deal of concern among riders who feel that they are not very good or that other riders are much better than they are. A strong, disciplined collecting ring steward who may, incidentally, also be the judge, will not allow any jockeying for position. She knows, just as much as you do, which are the skilled competitors and will try to get a good balance. Be prepared to do as you are told. You will, however, probably

Musical Mats in progress. A pony that leads willingly is essential in this game. The diagram shows the mats neatly laid out within a circle of cones. In practice, the mats may be scattered far more haphazardly and a good jockey makes a mental note of their position.

have a choice as to which lane you take. Here, you should be observant. If you are not in the first heat, watch what happens before it is your turn to enter the ring. Few gymkhana arenas are completely level and the playing field may have odd clumps of thistles or patches of longer, thicker grass. Some buckets and cones could be less stable than others. Try to choose a lane where the ground is even.

Finally – and this is a fact of which most riders, organisers and judges are unaware – note where the judge is placed. Most judging takes place at ground level and from this position it is almost impossible to tell in a close finish which rider finished first. An optical illusion always makes the rider furthest from the judge seem to be in front, even though she could be up to half a length behind. Unless the judge is raised on a platform or flatbed trailer, she will make this mistake. If you want to benefit from this, select the lane furthest from the judge.

Complaints

Should you – or should you not – complain? On the whole, the best advice is not to do so, although this does of course depend on the nature of the injury. If you disagree with the judge's decision, you have every right to feel aggrieved, but unless there has been a blatant miscarriage of justice your complaints will probably be ignored. In a Trotting Race, for example, if you think the winner cantered and failed to turn a circle, there is no fair way to right the wrong. In Ball and Bucket, if the winner's bucket does not contain the right number of balls, the best that the judge can do is to disqualify the winner and move everyone else up a place. It is unlikely that the race will be run again. Remember that mistakes can be made, even by judges, and while you may suffer today, tomorrow the mistake could be in your favour.

If the mistake concerns equipment – perhaps there are only three flags in your cone instead of four – you should be alert enough to point this out to the judge or stewards before the race begins. If you were chatting to your neighbour and only discovered the discrepancy when you came back to get the fourth flag, well, frankly, that is your fault.

Most shows have a rule governing objections. Usually, they have to be made in writing within thirty minutes of discovering the offence and accompanied by a deposit of anything between £5 and £15. The objection must be made by an adult on a junior competitor's behalf and, if it is overruled, the deposit will be forfeited. Objections, therefore, should not be made lightly. Usually, they concern the eligibility – or lack of it – of a pony or rider; the pony, for example, may be over height or the rider over age. You should be very certain of your facts before making an objection.

Objections against a judge's decision are unlikely to be upheld. Too often, the 'offence' is a matter of opinion – at the end of a day, everyone is too tired to get into an argument. If you say, 'It isn't fair!', the most likely answer you will get is, 'Well, life isn't fair!' And, at that, they are usually right.

Part 3

Becoming an Expert

Chapter One
From Pony Club to County Games

Joining the Pony Club offers the best chance of becoming really good at mounted games. This is, of course, not the only reason that most young riders pay their subscription every year and proudly wear their Pony Club badge and tie, but it can be a factor in your decision to fill in the enrolment form and look forward to receiving your programme of activities.

There are, however, many other benefits to be gained from being part of a games squad. Most riding competitions are, on the whole, individual activities. Your friends may be all around you but you are competing for yourself. If you make a mistake, you let down yourself and your pony. If you decide at the last minute not to enter, you may lose your entry fee but no one else is affected.

Games in the Pony Club, however, are essentially team efforts, and the benefits to a team member heavily outweigh the disadvantages.

When you first join the games squad, you are still very much an individual. Usually, you will find in your Pony Club programme or newsletter the name and telephone number of the team trainer, followed by a request for any member interested in the games to give her a ring. Unless you already know the trainer, it can be quite an ordeal for a young rider to pick up the telephone and ask to join the squad. It is important not to be nervous. Trainers are always looking for new blood, even if they have a very competent team already.

Generally, you will be told when practices take place and invited to attend the next one. You may have to persuade your parents to take you and your pony to the practice in a trailer unless the practice area is within hacking distance. In fact, it is a good thing to get parents involved. Parents in similar circumstances strike up friendships, get interested in the games and, before long, are offering to build equipment or act as line stewards in competitions.

You may find, unless you have a close friend who can join the squad at the same time as you, that you feel a little out of things at the first practice. You will probably not be very good or, at least, not as good as the old hands. The other children, who perhaps have been practising together for a long time, will have an easy relationship with one another and they will watch your performance both curiously and critically.

Do not be put off by this. They do not mean to shut you out. It is simply that, until you have attended a few practices, you are an outsider. Once you have shown, however, that you are determined to improve and to make one of the teams, you will find that you are being absorbed into the squad.

Suddenly, it will become important to you that everyone should do well, not only yourself. You will see the weaknesses in the squad and understand how the trainer is trying to overcome them. If she swaps riders about, it will be because one rider is better at that particular race than another and needs a faster pony. It is not necessarily a reflection on any rider's ability. Above all, you will find that you have become an important member of a group, striving together for the good of your branch. Older, more experienced members will spare the time to teach you the best way to tackle a race, showing you how to handle equipment, get your pony going faster and more accurately and in every way to improve your performance. You are now part of a team.

This is what team spirit is all about and it is what all the successful games teams have in abundance. It means that if team members quarrel – and most Pony Club branches will agree that this is not unknown – or the team trainer gets cross because somebody is late or is being lazy, in the end no one minds. On the day of the competition, they are one unit, desperate to do well for the sake of the team, quick to comfort if somebody makes a mistake.

A young rider who joins a games squad at, say, the age of nine, can have six years competing in Pony Club competitions. When, at last and usually with great regret, they get too old for Pony Club mounted games, many Pony Club members feel quite lost. There is no Area Final to work towards, no more practices to attend. Unless they switch their attention to other disciplines – show jumping, for example, or polo, or eventing – they are suddenly bereft. It is particularly hard if they have a really good gymkhana pony, especially one which still has plenty of competitive ability in him. Common sense suggests that the pony should be sold on, but his fifteen-year-old owner is not yet ready to do this. She may have acquired another pony or even a horse, one that is capable of tackling show jumping or cross-country at a higher level, but the old gymkhana pony still has a special place in her heart.

She also misses the games themselves: having honed her skills to perfection, she no longer has the competitions available in which to display them. Local gymkhanas are no use; to get any real satisfaction out of a good performance you need other people of similar ability to compete against.

It was the realisation that the end of every mounted games season saw several excellent performers shunted out into the cold that, several years ago, prompted the formation of the Mounted Games Association of Great Britain. The people behind its organisation had themselves long been connected with the Pony Club games. Moves to extend the age limit for games within the Pony Club had never come to anything, yet there were still heaps of teenagers about who did not feel ready to give up the games.

The new organisation offered these young people an extension. Games organisers all over the country were asked if they would be interested in helping, and many agreed. It was decided to divide the country according to county boundaries and to run competitions between county teams. No lower age limit was imposed, but twenty-one became the maximum. The MGAGB became very popular. In spite of the fact that inter-county competitions involved far more travelling than Pony Club ones and that standards were, if anything, higher than in the Pony Club, dozens of teenagers flocked to take part.

Most of the games played are the same as the Pony Club ones although they may be known by different names, so any fifteen-year-old contemplating the change should have little difficulty in making the transition.

The organisation also arranges something called The World Championships for individual performers. These are held annually around the country and are divided into age groups. Competitors do not have to belong to a society in order to compete; they simply make their own individual entries. The Championships are run over three days and are quite intensive. Competitors can arrange to camp at the showground and the event provides a great opportunity for games enthusiasts to meet old friends and make new ones. The standard of competition is, as might be expected, exceptionally high.

Not surprisingly, the ponies used by these older teenagers tend to be somewhat bigger than those used in Pony Club mounted games, an average of about 13.2 hands high as opposed to 12.2. The sense of enjoyment, however, remains the same.

Chapter Two
Choosing a Games Pony

A games pony is not like a show pony. It is not just a matter of finding one with the right conformation. It is not even a matter of choosing a particular breed. You cannot say that he must have small ears or a sloping shoulder, or that he must be Welsh rather than New Forest, or a Dartmoor pony rather than a crossbreed.

A good games pony is a proven pony – that is to say, he must have had the experience of playing games at a high level. If he has carried his young rider through to the Pony Club Zone Finals or, better still, to the Championships at Wembley, or if he is a regular competitor in county games, he is a valuable asset. First-class games ponies can change hands for thousands of pounds.

Most people, however, do not have thousands of pounds with which to buy a proven pony. The best they can hope for is to get a pony with potential, and it is the ability to judge potential that makes all the difference between success and failure.

Nevertheless, there are some guidelines to choosing a pony suitable for mounted games, and the following hints might help.

Size

The Pony Club lays down definite rules regarding the height of ponies permitted to take part in mounted games. Ponies bigger than 14.2 hands high are banned. On the other hand, ponies measuring 12.2 hands high or under are not allowed to be ridden in competitions by a child weighing more than 8 stone 5 lb (117 lb or 53 kg) dressed.

When it comes to size, therefore, it is your own build and athletic ability which must be taken into account.

On the whole, small ponies are more manoeuvrable but bigger ponies are faster. If you are a tall, thin featherweight, you can probably get away with a pony under 12.2 hh and you will be at an advantage when bending down to put a ball in a bucket or picking up litter on a stick. Getting on a small pony may be easier for you especially if all you have to do is fling one leg over the saddle and hop up. But remember that the more of a rider there is above the saddle the harder it is for a pony to balance himself properly and it will be more difficult for him to make tight turns.

Ponies near the upper height limit definitely have the edge in speed races. Even if they are unable to turn sharply round the final pole in the Bending Race, their speed as they flash in and out of the poles will soon leave the short-legged ponies behind. In the fastest races of all – the Sword Race and the Flag Race – a good large pony will always beat a good small one. With big ponies, however, getting off and, more importantly, getting on will always present problems.

If you are nine years old, reasonably fit, and hoping, with practice and hard work, to improve both your riding and your games skills, the best size to choose is around thirteen hands. Keen Pony Club members will find this size pony capable of a variety of Pony Club activities and, later on, when you need a horse capable of tackling horse trials and other cross-country events, you will still be able to ride your games pony at county level.

Remember, however, that this is only a guideline. Small, sturdy, strong ponies of native stock may not be fast but they are often agile, saving time when turning tightly round pieces of equipment, hugging the bending poles and allowing their athletic riders to retrieve fallen items without dismounting. Suppleness, balance and co-ordination are useful assets in the bigger ponies.

Conformation

Gymkhana ponies come in all shapes and sizes and you can ignore many of the points of conformation which would be considered faults in other spheres. A gymkhana pony does not have to be a pretty pony, and provided he has other qualities (particularly in temperament) it does not matter if his head is too large, his neck thin or his withers low. Check the width of his chest and girth. Games call for short bursts of energy and the pony should have ample room for his lungs to expand. A high

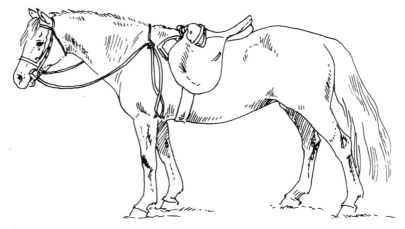

A nice sort of gymkhana pony, snaffle-mouthed and with strong quarters. Always knot your reins for mounted games: you need to have close control of your pony and, if you have to fumble for your reins, you will fumble the equipment as well.

head carriage is better, on the whole, than a low one because it helps a rider to get on and off at speed.

Temperament

Some people believe that this is the most important factor in any games pony, and it is true that whatever assets a pony possesses in other directions they are useless if his temperament is doubtful.

A pony must enjoy mounted games. This is easy to judge because he is bright-eyed and bouncy, keenly aware of every-thing that is going on, ready for anything.

He must be unflappable because he will be expected to face all manner of situations. Regardless of whether flags blow in his face, canes are waved near his head or balloons burst under his feet, he should stop when required and continue in a straight line when urged to do so. In team games, the biggest test of unflappability is during the hand-over of equipment from one rider to another. A pony which is next in line to take part must wait quietly while the other pony is charging towards him. His rider must have every chance to take the item from the incoming rider without worrying whether her pony will back off or shy away at the last moment.

Obedience

This is extremely important, especially if the pony is naturally fizzy and fast. This is not always easy to judge when trying out a pony for the first time, but if he responds to the aids and seems to have good co-ordination, training and practice can turn him into an excellent games pony.

Stopping when asked to do so and standing still until told to move off are actions which can make all the difference between winning and losing. Here again, training and practice can work wonders.

Under Pony Club rules, ponies must be ridden in a snaffle bit, although martingales and various types of dropped noseband are permitted. Not all ponies perform well in a snaffle, and for other activities they may well need a Pelham or a Kimblewick, but in a mounted games competition the choice of bit has to be a snaffle. Fortunately, enthusiastic games ponies soon learn when to stop and, even though their mouths may have hardened and their neck muscles thickened, they make excellent performers with a confident rider.

Age

A very young pony is not sufficiently developed to cope with the demands of mounted games, and for this reason the Pony Club will not allow ponies under four years of age to take part. However, even a four-year-old is still quite young and is certain to be inexperienced. If you are buying a pony specifically for gymkhanas, you would be wise to look for a pony that is at least eight years old.

Do not be in too much of a hurry to reject older ponies. There are many excellent games ponies around which are well into their twenties, making up in experience for what they might lack in suppleness and speed. Younger riders in particular can learn a great deal from a well-versed schoolmaster.

Willingness

A forward-going pony is essential, whether he is being used for high-powered competitions or merely for local shows. There is nothing more depressing for a rider than to have to kick and kick to get a stubborn pony out of a ponderous trot. A pony should be just as anxious to get to the far end of the arena as most ponies are to get back to the start. Nappiness may be the fault of the rider but at games level riders are more likely to suffer from inexperience and a nappy pony will not help.

It is a firm rule in all gymkhanas that a whip cannot be carried, and slapping a pony with the loop of the reins or even the palm of the hand is also forbidden. Using pieces of equipment as a whip incurs instant disqualification. Riders must therefore train their ponies to go forward at all times.

Other virtues

Because most gymkhana ponies are hardy, native types, their natural habitat is out of doors. Your pony should be easy to catch – there is nothing more frustrating than standing in a muddy field, shaking a scoop of nuts, while your pony circles a few yards away, just out of reach.

He should be easy to shoe – maintaining his feet in good condition is just as important in a games pony as in a high-powered eventer. He need not be shod but a farrier should make regular visits to trim the hooves and keep them in good shape.

He should also be easy to box. If you have a battle getting him into a trailer at the start of every show, neither of you will arrive on the ground in a fit state to give of your best. At the start of a competition, both you and your pony should be calm and confident.

Chapter Three
Keeping Fit

Someone once said that fitness is not just a matter of not being ill. Fitness means honing the body to a peak of strength, stamina, suppleness and well-being. There are no physical sports in which an unfit performer can beat a fit one. Riding is no exception.

Of all the disciplines in the riding world, mounted games probably benefits the most from a fit, athletic performer. No other riding competition requires so much from its participants in the way of stretching, bending, mounting, dismounting and running.

Some Pony Club branches insist that their mounted games squad should join a gymnastics class. If this sounds extreme, think how much easier it is to exercise under supervision. In a gymnastics class, you will learn how to make your body work for you, improving your flexibility and suppleness and toning up your muscles. You learn how to control your balance and co-ordination. All these help to improve your riding.

In all manner of games, the rider's athletic ability is important. The vault becomes easier, you will be able to bend low out of the saddle to scoop up litter or drop balls into buckets without over-balancing or upsetting your pony's balance. You learn to distribute your weight in the saddle so that you put less of a burden on your pony, and by your own suppleness you can use your weight to guide the pony.

There are exercises you can do at home to increase your level of fitness. Stretching exercises can be carried out on the back of the pony or on the ground.

Stretching exercises

On the ground
1 Lie on your back on a flat surface – your bedroom floor, for example – with your arms loosely at your sides and the palms of

Loosening and strengthening the muscles in your shoulders and arms. Swing each arm in turn in a circular movement.

your hands flat on the floor. With your left leg straight, bend your right leg at the knee. Now, from the hip, roll your right knee over your left thigh so that the knee just touches the floor. Roll back again. Try to keep your shoulders straight while you are doing this. Repeat the movement ten times, then rest for a moment before carrying out the same exercise with your left knee.

2 Stand with your feet slightly apart and raise your right arm above your head. Lean sideways until your left hand touches the outside of your left foot. Straighten up. Repeat ten times, then do the same thing on the other side.

3 Stand up straight, with both arms together above your head. Lean forward without bending your knees and touch the ground. Straighten up. Repeat several times.

Thigh and calf muscles can be strengthened and made more flexible by bending each leg in turn sharply at the knee and drawing it up till your heel touches your thigh. If your pony is not as well behaved as this one, ask a friend to hold his head.

4 Sit on the ground with your legs straight out and slightly apart. Your toes should point towards the ceiling. Lean forward and grasp the toe of your left foot with your right hand. Let your left arm swing out behind. Do the same with the opposite hand and foot. Alternate the movements several times, trying to keep a rhythm going.
5 Stand on one leg, grasp the knee of the other leg and bring it up to touch your forehead. This needs care to avoid over-balancing. Do this three times on each leg.

On your pony
1 Rise in your stirrups and stretch upwards with your arm

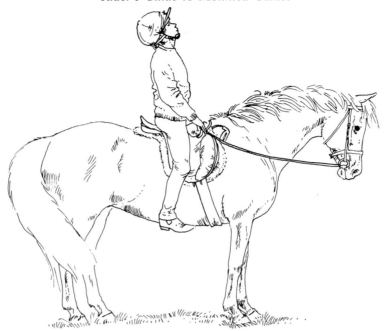

Stretching and improving the muscles of your back. Keep a hand on the pommel to steady yourself and stretch upwards as far as you can.

above your head. If necessary, steady yourself with the other hand on the pommel of the saddle. Lower yourself gently back into the saddle. Repeat several times, alternating the arms. Practise this exercise at first when the pony is stationary (if necessary, ask a friend to hold his head). Later, when you are sufficiently confident of your balance (when you no longer need to hold the pommel to steady yourself), try carrying out the exercise at a walk and then at a trot.

2 When the pony is moving, lean down and touch your right foot with your right hand. Then use the same hand to touch your left foot. Try this with the other hand.

3 Practise the scissors exercise, but make certain you have someone holding your pony at the time. In this exercise, you drop your reins. Place both hands on the pommel of the saddle, lean forward and swing your legs backwards and upwards. As they reach the top of the swing, take your weight on your hands, cross your legs and flip yourself round so that you end up facing backwards in the saddle. Repeat the exercise to bring yourself

back into the correct position. This is not an easy exercise as it depends on timing to be carried out successfully. But if you learn to do it well, it is a good basis on which to develop the vault.

Hand and eye co-ordination

First of all, check which is your dominant eye. To do this, hold your arm out straight and raise one finger. Line the finger up with some object – an ornament, a door handle, a picture, anything which is fairly prominent. Now close one eye. If the dominant eye is the one which remains open, your finger will still be in line with the object. If the closed eye is the dominant one, your finger will have moved in relation to the object.

Now practise on foot some of the task called for in mounted games. Plant a flag in a cone, place a ball on a cone, use a cane to spear a ring. Try to do this without checking.

Remember that these exercises can be carried out at any time, but it is best if you can do some of them every day. Never spend too long on exercising, and if you get tired stop immediately. And never force yourself. If at first, for example, you find that you cannot touch your toes, reach down as far as you can and exercise that way. After a few weeks, your suppleness will have increased so much that you *will* be able to reach your toes – a great triumph!

Part 4

Helping Others

Chapter One
Planning and Organising Gymkhanas

Anyone who has ever enjoyed a gymkhana has a great deal to offer the next generation. Fortunately for the future of horsemanship, the wish to help up-and-coming riders seems to be very strong and there are a great many people who are still involved in the riding scene even if they no longer ride themselves.

Running a gymkhana is an ideal introduction to organising competitions in general. This is because a gymkhana is usually an informal affair, without the need for qualified judges and money prizes, and, with running costs fairly low, it makes a good fund-raiser for charity. Quite apart from all that, running a gymkhana is fun.

If you decide to organise a show, the first thing you must do is to form an organising committee. It is, of course, possible to run a gymkhana single-handed but this puts a great deal of work on one person, and a small committee provides helpers and a sharing out of responsibility.

If you and your friends get together to organise the event, you must fix the date well in advance. This can be quite a problem in a keen riding area where there are many shows already established. Shows rely for success on their reputation, and people who regularly attend a particular show will not be tempted away to another event. These days, with such a variety of horsy activities, most weekends are already booked. A weekday in the school holidays may prove a better choice but remember, if you do choose a weekday, it could be difficult to find adult helpers who are not at work.

The Christmas holidays are not usually a good time. They are short, already occupied by Pony Club activities such as rallies, parties and Pony Club meets, and the gymkhana would need to be held indoors if you do not want to run the risk of cancellation in bad weather. Half-term breaks, at least in the winter and spring terms, are also out for much the same reason. This leaves the spring and summer holidays.

An April day is a good choice if you are lucky enough to live in an area where the ground is well-drained. On chalky soils, such as the South Downs, it is much easier to pick an early season date. Vehicles do less damage to the ground and farmers are more inclined to lend a field for the venue. On heavy, clay soils, few farmers will allow a show to take place on their land much earlier than mid-June.

The sooner you pick your date the more time you will have to plan the event properly. The first item to consider is advertising.

Advertising is a term covering all methods of making your gymkhana known about by those who are likely to attend. Local newspapers, including those which are given away free and exist entirely on their advertising revenue, usually have a section confined to horses. Some use a spring issue to publish a calendar of events for the coming season but, to be included in the calendar, you will almost certainly be expected to pay for a separate advertisement. To keep your costs down, you need not give more than the barest details – the name, date and place of the show and the promise that a schedule will be sent to anyone supplying a self-addressed, stamped envelope. You can, of course, add more details if you wish – starting time, for example, an indication of the different classes which will be held, the charity or organisation to which proceeds will be given – but the announcement will cost you more.

This should be sufficient to reach all the neighbouring riders. You can reinforce it by putting posters up around the area. Home-made posters can be very eye-catching, especially if they bear an attractive design or a colourful logo. Anyone on your committee who is good at drawing will be able to produce them, and the cost of the paper can be added to expenses.

Finally, the schedules you produce can themselves be used as advertisements. Distribute them among saddlers and feed-merchants in your district so that would-be entrants can pick one up when they go to buy a new hoofpick or order pony nuts. Leave them in the local shop or post office. And remember to monitor them on a weekly basis, supplying a few more when the first lot run out.

Nearer the date of your show, you can take schedules to other shows. The secretary's table at these events nearly always carries a pile of schedules for shows in the future, and most of them get snapped up.

Of course, supplying schedules to shops and shows implies that you have already drawn up your programme. Planning the schedule, in fact, is the next task after planning your advertising campaign; it is also the most important because it is the content of your schedule which makes riders decide to enter your show rather than another one on the same day.

The classes you choose are dependent on the equipment you have or can borrow and you should consider them very carefully.

First of all, how many sections or age groups do you propose?

Leading-rein classes are always popular but you have to decide what age limit to impose. The most popular ceiling for leading-rein riders is eight years old, on the grounds that anyone over that age should be able to manage a pony by themselves. But some children do not take up riding until they are already eight or more and you may have a number of nine- or ten-year-olds in your district who lack the confidence to compete without a handler. On the other hand, if you do extend the age limit, the bigger children will almost certainly have the edge on the tinies, not only in events where the riders have to run to the winning post but also in manipulating items of equipment. It is very difficult to decide what is the best solution. If you have both the time and the resources, it is worth considering dividing the leading-rein classes into two sections, confining the very small children to events on their own.

At this point, you should also consider members of Riding for the Disabled groups. The benefits of riding to disabled people of all ages are not in question: contact with horses and ponies has a marked effect on both the mental and physical welfare of these riders. For children especially, it enables them to join their peers in activities which many people once thought were quite beyond them. Depending on the games you select for the leading-rein sections, RDA riders can join in and compete on level terms. For RDA members, therefore, it is reasonable to waive the upper age limit.

However, you may be asked if an older RDA member – a teenager, for example – may enter the section for other children of his or her age group. As a general rule, it is not a good idea to mix leading-rein riders with riders off the leading rein, the reason being that a led rider (who does not have to worry about controlling her pony) is at an advantage. But where a led rider is disabled, this advantage by and large is diminished and you can probably safely agree to an exception being made.

81

In Part I, Chapter 1 you will find many games listed that are suitable for leading-rein riders. When selecting events for your leading-rein classes, try to make a good mix, choosing one or two events which require some dexterity from the child as well as one or two which depend solely on luck.

Deciding age groups for riders off the leading rein is subject to your own knowledge of the children who ride in your area. Most shows confine themselves to two sections, one for children aged, say, twelve years and under, the other for riders over twelve and up to and including sixteen. Some organisers do not actually define an age group for the second of these sections, merely describing it is as 'open'. If you opt for this description, bear in mind that 'open' means exactly what it says – open to everybody, regardless of age, provided they do not have to be led. This includes all those riders who are eligible for the twelve-and-under group. If you do not want them to enter both sections but you do want adults to feel free to join in, then label the third section thirteen years and over.

A word of warning here. It is easy to get carried away when drawing up a schedule and to place six or more events in each section and add an extra section for good measure, so that you end up with thirty separate games. Spare a thought for the gymkhana judge and her helpers. With more than six entries in a class, heats and a final have to be held; more than twelve entries and the number of heats rises to three. If you are not careful, you may be asking your judge to preside over a hundred or more different heats until both she and the arena party are on their knees. It is better to confine each section to four events and then to plan the running order so that equipment can be erected and removed with the minimum of stress.

Always consider equipment when defining the events. Some equipment is easy to make but difficult or time-consuming to erect. Other items take a while to gather together, but once acquired can be used time and time again. Bending poles, for example, may be bought reasonably cheaply from a local timber merchant but, in summer when the ground is hard, can be difficult to set up. Washing-up liquid containers for use in a litter race, on the other hand, can take several months to amass, even when everyone you know is pressed into saving their empty containers. Cones have to be bought (yes, it is both illegal and dangerous to remove them from the highway) and, if your resources are slender, they may be more than you can afford.

However, once purchased, provided they are looked after they will last for years.

Consumables – that is, potatoes (for a potato race) or apples (for apple-bobbing) – are items which must be bought anew every time the event is held. For an end-of-season show, however, especially in a good apple year, it is usually possible to gather as many windfalls as you want. Under those circumstances, therefore, apple-bobbing becomes a cheap game to include. But you will, of course, need water, which means taking it to the arena in suitable containers.

If, as often happens, your show is a huge success and becomes a regular feature of the horsy year, you will in time build up a useful collection of equipment. By this time your choice of events will be much wider but you will also be such an old hand at the planning of a gymkhana you will no longer need this book.

The simplest solution of all is to borrow equipment if you can. Try and find out who provides the equipment at other shows and see if you can arrange to borrow both the games items and their owner. The trainer of your local Pony Club mounted games squad is a possible source, although bear in mind that since most of the items will have been bought out of branch funds the branch itself may be reluctant to lend them to any event outside the branch's jurisdiction. The other drawback to borrowing from the Prince Philip Cup squad is that, unless the branch is in the habit of organising mounted games competitions, the number of items possessed by the trainer may be sufficient only for one or two lanes. This is no good for a gymkhana where you must have enough to furnish at least seven lanes.

Once you are satisfied that you have the equipment for all manner of games – remember that games which call for absolutely no equipment (like walk, trot and canter or trotting races) are also very difficult to judge – you can then go ahead with placing them in your schedule and settling on the running order.

The logistics of the running order are something that many show organisers overlook. Always picture to yourself where all the items of equipment will be when one game has finished and the next is due to begin. Bending poles, for example, which need time to erect should feature early on in the programme. They can then be put up in advance. If poles have to be removed at any point, schedule poleless classes to come after those which need poles. It is time-wasting to have to put poles back up again and consequently frustrating for the competitors, not to mention hard work for helpers. Of course, flattened or broken poles must always be straightened or replaced.

When you have decided on the gymkhana events, you must consider what other competitions you can provide. Jumping is universally popular, especially if you can keep the height of the fences reasonably low so that novice or nervous riders can be encouraged to have a go. It is best to set the jumps up in a separate ring, using them for Clear Round Jumping during the first two or three hours of the day. Clear Round Jumping is a great money-spinner. Riders pay at the collecting ring (usually £1 or £1.50 at a time) for the right to tackle the course. If they go clear, their reward is a rosette; some riders with difficult ponies will spend anything up to £10 or more attempting to win a rosette. You can start the day with a tiny course of jumps measuring eighteen inches or less, which gives the chance of a rosette to very young riders or children on the leading rein, and gradually raise the fences to a maximum of about two feet six inches.

State on the schedule the height of the jumps and the time when they will be raised. Make it very clear that riders should pay entry fees at the ringside. It should also be stressed in the schedule when the proper jumping competitions will begin. If you are too vague, you will find that riders are still queuing up for their clear round attempts just when you are anxious to get on with the rest of the programme.

The choice of jumping competitions is entirely up to you. You may decide to stick to straightforward contests, open perhaps only to novice riders, in which competitors with clear rounds or equality of faults jump off over a shortened course against the clock. Or you may stage more unusual classes: Bareback Jumping, Take Your Own Line, Ace-King-Queen-Jack, Scurry Jumping, Baton Relay or Pony and Dog Jumping.

The rules for these 'fun' classes are fairly straightforward but make certain the competitors know the rules before they start. If you have room on your schedule, you can print a description of each class; if not, try to pin it up near the secretary's box where everybody can read it.

Just in case *you* are not certain of the rules, here are some guidelines:

Bareback jumping

Riders compete without saddles over a simple course. Jump-offs are against the clock. The drawback of this class is that many riders, especially those who are likely to come to your gymkhana, are probably not very confident at jumping with a saddle, let alone without one. Safety is an important factor: bareback riders fall off more easily.

Take Your Own Line

This usually consists of a single round against the clock, the rider with the fewest faults and the fastest round being the winner. Each fence must be jumped once only but from any direction and it is important to design a good riding course with fences that can be tackled from either side. Thus, you should not have a triple or a double which includes a spread. Parallels are out because the far side of a parallel must be a single pole. Confine spreads to double oxers and take care not to create false ground lines. As a competition it is a good means of teaching riders to consider their jumping performance as a whole: they have to work out an economical line to take without asking their ponies to approach jumps from an impossible angle.

Ace-King-Queen-Jack

This is another class where fences should be jumpable from any direction. All the fences in the course are used but are graded in height, and each fence is given a points value which should be clearly visible on each jump. Usually, every jump except four are invitingly low; the remaining four – the Ace, King, Queen and Jack of the class's title – are bigger and have higher values, the biggest being the Ace. This jump could be two feet nine inches in height, or even three feet. To encourage competitors to jump a sensible course, do not make the difference in points too large: the small jumps, for example, could be worth five points, the other four seven, eight, nine and ten points respectively. Competitors should feel that they can gain plenty of points by taking a flowing route rather than jumping backwards and forwards over the same fence. Your show jumping judges need to be carefully briefed on the rules, and it might be a good idea to equip them with a calculator. Each rider is given one minute to jump as many jumps as possible and is awarded the appropriate points for every fence negotiated successfully. If a fence is refused the only penalty is time; if it is knocked down, no points are awarded, it is not rebuilt and cannot therefore be jumped again. The clock should start when the bell is sounded, and the bell is rung again when time is up. The rider should jump one more fence after the final signal is heard. The winner is the rider who has gained the most points.

Scurry Jumping

Here the rider jumps a set course, starting when the bell is sounded and finishing when the bell rings again. Each rider should be allowed, say, one minute. If they complete the course within the time limit, they start a second round. Jumps negotiated successfully are counted; jumps knocked down on the first round cannot be jumped a second time. The winner is the rider who clears the most jumps. The disadvantage of this class is that more than one rider may reach the same part of the course in the time allowed and placings may then have to be shared.

Baton Relay

This is a pairs class and often quite popular. Riders can enter themselves as a pair beforehand or you can team up individual riders on the day. Both riders have to negotiate the same course but not together. They enter the ring together and the second rider takes up a holding position somewhere near the final jump. The first rider, who must carry a whip, sets off on her round at the ring of a bell. When she has finished, she hands the whip to the second rider who then follows the same course. If a fence is knocked down by the first rider, the second should be signalled to wait before she starts her round and the clock is stopped while the jump is rebuilt. If the first rider has three refusals, she immediately hands the whip to the second rider who takes over at the fence where the third refusal occurred, completes the first round and then continues on her own round. The two rounds and the hand-over are timed and the fastest pair with the fewest faults are the winners. Any time taken in rebuilding a jump is noted and deducted from the total. Should the second rider get three refusals, both riders are eliminated.

Pony and Dog Jumping

This is another popular class but does require extra equipment and work on the part of the organisers. Alongside each pony jump, a smaller dog jump must be erected. This can be made of a lightweight pole balanced on cones or blocks; straw bales or old motor tyres can also be used. The rider negotiates the pony course first, dismounts and hands the pony to a steward. She must then complete the dog course on foot, accompanied by a dog on a leash, the dog of course jumping the fences. The two rounds are timed. If preferred, the dog handler can be another child or a parent. The winners are the pony/dog combination which finishes the course in the shortest time.

Having decided what gymkhana events your show is going to have, and having settled on the jumping classes, you can add one more extremely popular event – Handy Pony. Like Clear Round Jumping, Handy Pony should be entered and paid for on the day. The Handy Pony judge needs a pad, pencil and stopwatch. This class needs a separate ring, and it is wise to state on the schedule the period when the class is open. Handy Pony is in effect an obstacle course which riders negotiate against the clock. They pay at the ringside and can have as many goes as they like as long as they pay an entry fee (say, £1 or £1.50) each time. The judge records their time and at the end announces the placings. Riders can get very competitive over this class, especially if they think they have managed a good time. Those in contention will return again and again to see if anyone else has beaten them and to have another go. All this swells the funds very satisfactorily.

The obstacles can be as difficult or ingenious as you like. The following list shows a number of different hazards and may give you inspiration. All of them have been included in Handy Pony classes at different times.

1. Erect three or four bending poles about five metres apart. The rider must weave in and out from one end to the other.
2. Set up two 'tables' – upturned swing bins, dustbins or oil drums. Place a basket on one and two or three tins of baked beans on the other. Competitors must pick up the basket, ride to the 'shop', collect the 'shopping' and return with it to the table.
3. Put up a washing line. This can consist of binder twine strung between two poles. Peg out four garments. The rider picks up a laundry basket, collects the washing and replaces the basket at the start.
4. Take a piece of old carpet measuring at least 1.5 by 4 metres. Lay it out on the ground, weighting it down with straw

bales. The competitor must ride or lead her pony over the carpet between the bales.

5 Build a gate, which must be opened by the rider, who passes through and shuts the gate before going on to the next obstacle.

6 Set up a simple jump, such as crossed poles, which the rider must negotiate successfully.

7 Use two cones, placed ten metres apart. Balance a tennis ball on top of one. The rider must carry the ball from one cone to the other.

8 Place a hat, scarf and pyjama jacket on a straw bale. The rider must dress up in the garments, putting the hat, of course, on top of her riding hat, ride to another straw bale and remove the clothes.

9 Set up several empty cans on a table or straw bale. Place another straw bale or table three metres away. This second table should have a supply of small bean bags or rolled-up socks. The rider must dismount and throw the missiles at the cans. When three have been knocked down, she remounts and continues to the next obstacle.

10 Borrow a front-unload trailer and park it in the ring. Lower both front and rear ramps. The pony must be led through the trailer.

11 Place a cow-bell on a table or upturned bin. The rider must pick up the bell and ring it. This is quite a good hazard to finish with, signalling to the judge that the course has been completed and the watch should be stopped.

There are no doubt additional ideas that you can come up with, many of them involving transferring equipment from one container or table to another. You and the judge should decide beforehand on the penalties for failing to negotiate an obstacle or for knocking down a jump. Adding on time is usually the best solution, such as five seconds for the knockdown and twenty seconds for failing, say, to walk through the trailer after three attempts.

Remember that only the rider's best time counts towards the final placings.

Printing the schedule

Getting a schedule printed has become much easier with the development of word processors, computers and photocopiers. A simple schedule can be typed out on A4 paper although more elaborate ones are not too difficult or expensive to produce. Make certain that general rules and any age or height limits are clearly stated.

The front of the schedule should look something like this:

KINGSLEY & DISTRICT
GYMKHANA & JUMPING SHOW
at HOME FARM, KINGSLEY

by kind permission of Mrs & Mrs R. Smith

on Saturday 24 July 1995
First event: 9.30 a.m.

Organising Committee
George Smith
Rosemary Anderson
Gemma Briggs
William Smith

Hon. Secretary
Susan Long
Woodbine Cottage
Kingsley
Tel. 0004 687913

Refreshments: Sunnyside Catering
First aid: British Red Cross
Loudspeaker: Kingsley Communications Ltd

Entries close Wednesday, 21 July. Late entries: £1 extra

Inside, the schedule of classes might read:

Ring One   Gymkhana events   9.30 a.m.
Section A (Leading rein: 10 years & under)
1 Mug Race
2 Musical Mats

  3 Crossing the River
  4 Flag Race
Section B (Off leading rein: 12 years & under)
  5 Bending
  6 Flag Race
  7 Sock & Bucket Race
  8 Obstacle Race
Section C (Off leading rein: over 12 years)
  9 Obstacle Race
10 Bending
11 Flag Race
12 Sock & Bucket Race

Entry fees: £1 per class or £3.50 per section.
Rosettes to 6th place. Victor Ludorum trophy in each section.

Ring Two   Handy Pony
10 a.m to 1 p.m.
Entry fee: £1.50. Pay as you enter at ringside.
Rosettes to 6th place in each age group.

Ring Three   Jumping
Clear Round Jumping 9.30 a.m. to 12 noon.
Height of jumps: 18in. to 2ft. Jumps will be raised every hour.
Entry fee: £1.50. Pay as you enter at ringside.
Clear round rosette awarded for each clear round.

13 Minor Jumping (for Rider/Pony Combination never to have won a
    jumping class). Riders 12 years & under. Height of jumps: approx.
    2ft.
Entry fee £2. Rosettes to 6th place.

14 Novice Jumping (for Rider/Pony Combination never to have won
    a jumping class). Riders over 12 years. Height of jumps: approx.
    2ft 6in.
Entry fee £2. Rosettes to 6th place.

15 Ace–King–Queen–Jack. Riders any age.
Entry fee £2. Rosettes to 6th place.

16 Baton Relay Pairs Jumping. Riders any age. Height of jumps: 2ft
    6in. max.

Entry fee £4 per pair. Rosettes to 6th place.

17 Rider and Dog Jumping. Riders any age; dog any breed. Entry fee £3. Rosettes to 6th place.

General Rules

1 The judge's decision is final.

2 All entries must be accompanied by the correct remittance and are received on condition that the Organisers accept no responsibility for any loss, damage or injury etc. which, may be sustained by persons, horses, vehicles or property whatsoever.

3 The Organisers reserve the right to change or cancel classes and reduce the number of rosettes awarded in classes with fewer than six entries. They also reserve the right to disqualify or refuse the entry of any competitor for any reason deemed fit.

4 No horse or pony under four years of age may take part.

5 No horse or pony may be ridden more than once in any class, except in Clear Round Jumping and Handy Pony.

6 Correct dress must be worn at all times. Hard hats, with chinstraps fastened, must be worn when riders are mounted, both inside and outside the ring.

7 No entry money can be refunded unless a vet's or doctor's certificate accompanies the claim.

8 Objections, if any, can be lodged only by a competitor or by a parent or guardian. The objection must be in writing and accompanied by a deposit of £10 not later than half-an-hour after the occurrence which gave rise to it, or, in the case of an objection to the eligibility of a competitor, not later than the end of the class. The deposit will be returned if the objection is upheld.

9 No whips or spurs may be worn, except in the Jumping Classes.

10 All dogs must be kept on a lead.

11 The age of the competitor is taken as on the day of the show.

12 Riders in leading-rein classes may not enter any other class off the leading rein.

13 Winners of challenge trophies will be asked to leave a deposit of £5, refundable when the trophy is returned.

14 The Organisers have taken reasonable precautions to ensure the health and safety of everyone present. For these measures to be effective, everyone must take all reasonable precautions to avoid and prevent accidents occurring and

must obey the instructions of the Organisers and all Officials and Stewards.

Do not forget to include an entry form in each schedule. The entry form should look like this:

KINGSLEY & DISTRICT GYMKHANA AND JUMPING SHOW ENTRY FORM

Name of Rider	*Age*	*Name of Pony*	*Entry Fee*
		Red Cross donation	50p
		Total	

Name ....
Address...
....
....
....
Tel. No ....

Cheques should be made payable to
Kingsley & District Gymkhana
Send your entry form, with remittance, to:
Susan Long, Woodbine Cottage, Kingsley. Tel. 0004 687913
Entries close Wednesday, 21 July. Late entries £1 extra.

There are one or two aspects of the schedule which should be explained. Rules 2 and 14, for example, are both disclaimers and are there to discourage anyone suffering an injury at your show from suing you for damages. They do not, however, absolve you totally from responsibility, and a wise organising committee will take out insurance against possible claims for compensation.

The best plan is to consult an insurance broker. If you do not know one, look in the Yellow Pages under the appropriate section for the name and address of a local broker. A privately run gymkhana should be covered against two forms of liability: **public liability** describes the organisers' responsibility for injury and/or damage to third parties and their property caused by negligence on the part of the organisers and their helpers and stewards; **contractual liability** is accepted by the organisers when the gymkhana is held in a public place, such as a public park. It indemnifies the owners of the park against any claim made against them for public liability and, furthermore, covers the cost of making good any damage caused by the gymkhana. The premium is not usually very high but it should be regarded as a necessary expense.

First aid cover is another essential expense. At most shows held in Great Britain, this can be provided by one of two organisations: the British Red Cross and St John Ambulance Brigade. Both offer skilled first aid cover and their helpers, who are volunteers, are highly trained. Again, if you do not know the name of the local organiser, look in the Yellow Pages. Ring the organiser and explain what sort of show you are organising and give an estimate of the number of riders you expect to attend. You will be expected to pay a fee or make a donation, and the presence of an ambulance will cost you more than, say, having two qualified first-aiders on foot. Since their presence is of benefit to the competitors, many shows nowadays impose a small charge, shown on the entry form and payable with the entry fees.

Some form of public address system is necessary for the success of a show. It is the only means by which you, as organiser, can keep in touch with competitors and spectators, and it is vital to the smooth running of a show. Some providers of PA systems can offer a number of useful extras – commentary box with bell and timing devices, telephone connection to the collecting ring steward, and a cassette player for playing music over the amplifier. Always get the best you can afford.

In an all-day show, however modest, competitors and spectators alike will appreciate the chance of buying refreshments. It is possible to arrange for mobile caterers to attend your show; in return they will make a small contribution towards your funds. However, if it is possible to organise the refreshments yourselves, you will make more money. Very simple refreshments can be sold from the back of an estate car: canned drinks, chocolate bars and individually wrapped biscuits can all be sold at a profit. There is room at the rear of an empty horsebox or cattle truck for more elaborate equipment – a camping stove for frying bacon for bacon sandwiches (always immensely popular), or an urn for boiling water for tea, coffee or soup. Disposable cups and plates dispense with the need to wash up, but remember to lay on plenty of rubbish bags.

Lavatories must also be provided at a show. The cost of these varies greatly. The type that look like individual telephone boxes are usually quite expensive; it is often cheaper to hire a trailer or converted caravan. To find out where you can obtain them, look under Mobile Toilets in the Yellow Pages. Enquire about them well in advance – inexpensive units get booked up very quickly.

Stakes and rope are needed for defining the arenas. Metal stakes are the easiest to erect but chestnut fencing posts can be used. The rope should be thick enough to be readily visible, and brightly coloured for the same reason. Do not use binder twine which may be colourful but cannot be seen very easily. Stakes and rope often present the greatest problem for show organisers; if you do not know where to get them from, ask the secretaries of neighbouring shows or try your local branch of the Pony Club.

Finally, make certain that you have plenty of stewards and other helpers. You will need help beforehand – putting up rings and equipment and erecting jumps – on the day and with the clearing up afterwards. If possible, put individual members of your committee in charge of the different stages, telling them to arrange their own working parties. It is very important to the efficient running of your show to delegate; if you try to do everything yourself, things will get overlooked and you will wear yourself out. The following is a checklist of everything that needs to be done to ensure a successful gymkhana.

1 Form a committee.
2 Decide venue and date.
3 Check that the venue you have chosen is available.
4 Draw up a schedule and arrange for it to be printed.
5 Ring up judges and confirm with a letter and schedule.
6 Book PA equipment.
7 Book mobile lavatories.
8 Book Red Cross or St John Ambulance Brigade.
9 Arrange insurance.

10 Arrange catering.

11 Arrange to borrow a tent, caravan or trailer for use as a secretary's office on the day of the show.

12 Advertise the show.

13 Distribute schedules around saddlers, corn chandlers etc.

14 Arrange to borrow jumps, stakes, rope and gymkhana equipment.

15 Open building society account.

16 Work out the number of rosettes you will need (usually available from manufacturers in sets of six) and add three or four additional sets as spares or to have handy in case of a tie. Do not forget to order a few specials – children in leading-rein classes normally get a rosette each. Order at least a hundred Clear Round rosettes, preferably in a variety of colours as this encourages rosette winners to have more than one go. If you are awarding trophies for points winners, you may wish to give a championship rosette as well. Order these and any championship runners-up rosettes at the same time. Rosettes can be single-tiered or more and the price depends on the number of tiers, the closeness of the pleating and the length of the tails, the more tiers, the tighter the pleating and the longer the tails all adding to the cost. The cheapest rosettes of all are what are known as 'stock' ones, which means that the centre disc is printed with the placing but does not carry the name of the individual show. The colour or colours if two- or three-tiered rosettes are chosen does not affect the cost. The usual colours chosen for the different places are:

Position	Ordinary Shows	Pony Club Shows
1st	Red	Blue
2nd	Blue	Red
3rd	Yellow	Green
4th	Green	Yellow
5th	Orange or Pink	Pink
6th	Mauve or Brown	Mauve
Highly Commended	White or Pale Blue	White
Special	Pink or Lilac	Pink

Make certain that you put your order in early and, if you do not receive an acknowledgement within ten days, check that your order has been received. After that, leave it to the manufacturers to send the rosettes in time for your show. They are usually very reliable.

17 Check equipment. Arrange to borrow or make any items you are short of. Always have enough for seven lanes. If you get only seven

entries in one class and six rosettes are being awarded, it is not possible to run two heats. It is better to run all seven entries in one race.

18 Relax and wait for the entries to come rolling in.

19 About three weeks prior to the show, telephone last year's winners of challenge trophies and remind them that the cups must be returned.

Three days before the show

20 Organise and co-ordinate a working party to set up rings and equipment. It may be necessary to ask an adult with a towing vehicle to collect a trailer-load of jumps, but it is equally important to have several strong and enthusiastic helpers available to unload and erect the jumps.

End of the show

21 Try to see that enough people stay behind to help you clear up. An appeal over the loudspeaker can be very effective in recruiting volunteers. Dismantling one ring can begin as soon as all the classes in it have finished even though there may still be classes to complete in other rings. Parents are usually willing to lend a hand if they know that you need assistance.

22 When you get home, collect all your papers together in order and put them in a folder in a safe place. The number of entries in each class will help you next year when it comes to drawing up another schedule. You also need to collate the results and, if you wish, write or type them out for the local paper. Record the names and telephone numbers of challenge cup winners. At the end of the show you may feel that you will never forget, but in twelve months' time it will be a different story.

23 Put away any unused rosettes for next year.

24 Count the money! If you have made a good profit, decide how much to give the club or charity for which the money has been raised. If possible, reserve enough of the proceeds to give you a good base for next year.

Chapter Two
Games to Choose

Helping to train a Prince Philip squad offers plenty of satisfaction; it is also a good way of giving back to the Pony Club some of the benefits you yourself gained from being a member. The games played are selected each year by the Pony Club's Games Committee: unless they are new inventions, they will have been played sometime in the past, probably by you when you were in the team.

When you organise a gymkhana, the choice of games is up to you. Always try to seek a good balance and, if possible, plenty of variety. The following games, listed in alphabetical order, gives the rules most commonly in use: there may be small local variations. Always make sure that your gymkhana judges know exactly what rules you wish to operate.

Apple-bobbing

Objective: The rider has to retrieve an apple from a bucket of water, using only her teeth.
Equipment for each lane: Bucket, half-filled with water, containing an apple, placed at the far end of the arena.
Method: Each competitor rides to the bucket, dismounts and collects the apple with her teeth. She then remounts and rides to the finish.
Drawbacks: Containers of water are heavy and cumbersome. Apples may have to be bought. Some people think that this is a dangerous race as the quickest way to secure the apple is to plunge your head into the water and anchor the apple on the bottom. To do this, most riders remove their hats; this means that a rider is kneeling on the ground, close to her pony's feet, without any protective headgear.
Firm rules: If the hat is removed, it must be replaced and the chinstrap secured before the rider remounts.

Be prepared to get wet in the Apple Bobbing Race. Submerging your head in the bucket is the only way to pick up the apple with your teeth. Remember to replace your hat and fasten the chinstrap before remounting.

Aunt Sally

Objective: To knock down old baked bean cans which have been balanced on a table or bale of straw using rolled-up socks or small bean bags as missiles. The number of cans to be knocked down should be specified in the schedule.

Equipment for each lane: One straw bale, table or upturned bin, each bearing four or five cans. Upturned bin set two to three metres from the cans; eight to twelve rolled-up socks or small bean bags.

Method: Rider goes as fast as possible to the bin bearing the missiles, dismounts and shies socks at the tins. When the appropriate number (usually three) has been knocked down, she remounts and returns to the finish.

Drawbacks: Requires several members of an arena party to set up the equipment and a line steward or judge for each lane to retrieve missiles and check that competitors stay at the required distance from the cans.

Ball, Sock or Potato and Bucket

Objective: To collect a number of balls, socks or potatoes from the far end of the arena, one at a time, and drop them into a bucket.

Equipment for each lane: Bucket set up halfway down the arena. Three, four or five tennis balls, rolled-up socks or potatoes placed in a heap on the ground at the far end.

Method: The competitor rides to the pile of socks, balls or potatoes, dismounts and retrieves one. She then remounts and rides to the bucket where she drops the sock inside. The remaining socks, etc., must be transferred to the bucket in the same way. When all are in the bucket, she rides to the finish.

Firm rules: If the ball, sock or potato misses the bucket or bounces out, the rider must dismount to replace it. She does not have to remount to do this, but must be back astride her pony before returning to fetch another ball. Only one item may be placed in the bucket at any one time. Similarly, a bucket knocked over must be set up again and its contents restored.

Bend down as low as you can when placing a sock or ball in a bucket. This rider would be wiser to reverse her hand when releasing the ball. By holding her hand palm forward, as she is here, she runs the risk of unwittingly throwing the ball which could cause it to miss the bucket or bounce out.

As with Sock and Bucket, the closer you can get to where the ball has to be placed the better. In this picture, the rider is collecting the ball from the cone in Ball and Cone but she needs to bend just as sharply when depositing the ball.

Ball and Cone

Objective: To place a tennis ball on a cone at the far end of the arena and to pick up another one from a cone placed centrally.
Equipment for each lane: Two cones, one on the centre line, one at the far end. Two tennis balls, one of which is placed on the centre cone while the other is handed to the rider before the start.
Method: The rider places the ball on the empty cone and picks up the other on the way home.
Firm rules: If a cone is knocked over, a ball falls or the rider fails to collect one on her way to the winning line, she must correct the error.

Picking up a tennis ball in the Ball and Cone Race. Note how far the rider is leaning over, never taking her eye off the ball for one moment.

Ball and Racquet

Objective: To carry a tennis ball balanced on a tennis racquet up and down a line of bending posts. The rider is not allowed to touch the ball or miss out a post. Dropped balls may be replaced from a spare store.

Equipment for each lane: Three bending posts set eight to ten yards (7.3 to 9.1 metres) apart. Small container set on top of the centre pole containing three tennis balls. Tennis racquet with a crosspiece fixed to the handle, projecting three inches (7.3 centimetres) on either side. Fourth ball.

Method: At the start, the rider is given a tennis racquet and a ball, which she balances on the head of the racquet. At the signal to start she bends up and down the poles, carrying the racquet. The ball may only be touched by hand if the rider has dropped one and has to retrieve another, but as soon as the ball is back on the racquet head the rider's hand must hold the racquet behind the crosspiece.

Drawbacks: Equipment is difficult to make and may be expensive to buy. As this is an established Pony Club game, however, it may be possible to borrow adapted racquets from the Pony Club trainer.

Firm rules: Riders may continue to replace dropped balls from the store in the container on the centre pole. If all the balls have been used, however, the rider must dismount and retrieve a dropped ball.

Balloon Bursting

Objective: To burst balloons attached to a board or sack on the ground.

Equipment for each lane: Board or sack on centre line. Three or more inflated balloons attached to the board or sack with pegs. Bamboo cane, four feet (1.2 metres) long, with a pin taped to one end, placed in a cone, pin down, at the far end.

Method: The rider collects the cane with the pin, returns to the balloons and bursts a stipulated number. She then rides to the finish.

Drawbacks: Equipment takes time to prepare. At an ordinary gymkhana, some ponies may be frightened by bursting balloons. This is another popular Prince Philip Cup game, and ponies which have had practice at this event are usually unmoved by the balloons.

Bursting balloons in the Balloon Race. This picture shows clearly how short the pony's reins are, enabling his rider to have close control.

102

Beaker Race

Objective: To transfer plastic beakers from separate bending poles and pile them on another pole.
Equipment for each lane: Four bending poles in line. Three plastic beakers inverted on the tops of the second, third and fourth poles.
Method: Rider collects each beaker in turn and stacks them one on top of the other on the first pole.
Firm rules: Beakers may be collected in any order. If one is dropped, the rider must remount before stacking it on the first pole. If the stack falls, the rider may replace the beakers from the ground.

Bending

Objective: To weave up and down a line of bending poles in the least possible time.
Equipment for each lane: Four to six bending poles set up seven to ten yards (6.4 to 9.1 metres) apart.
Method: Competitors weave in and out of the poles, up the arena and back again. The first pole may be passed on the left or the right.
Firm rules: If a rider misses a pole, she must correct her mistake by returning to the point where the error occurred and picking up the race again at that point. If a pole is broken, the rider is disqualified.
Safety note: Bending poles should be at least four-and-a-half feet (1.35 metres) tall and as thick as a broom handle. Do not use bamboo canes which may splinter if broken and could cause injury to a pony. Metal stakes are also unsuitable.

Bottle Race

Objective: To place a bottle on an upturned bin at the far end of the arena and pick up another from a similar bin on the centre line.
Equipment for each lane: Two upturned bins (swingbin size). Two plastic lemonade bottles, weighted with sand, one of which is given to the rider at the start.

Method: The rider must place the bottle upright on the bin at the far end. Collecting the second bottle may be carried out at any speed.

Firm rules: Fallen bottles or bins knocked over must be picked up before the rider continues.

Canter, Trot and Walk

Objective: To complete the race at a canter, trot and walk, changing pace at specified points.

Equipment for each lane: Marker cone or pole at each end of the arena.

Method: Each rider canters – or gallops – to the far cone, goes round it and returns to the near cone. She then trots to the far end, rounds it and walks to the finish.

Drawbacks: This is an exceptionally difficult race to judge fairly unless you have a judge assigned to each lane. One person cannot possibly watch every rider at the same time, and the rider who fails to turn a circle may be missed. It is very embarrassing at the end of the race to be told by spectators that the winner had not complied with the rules. It can also be quite difficult with a bouncy pony to judge whether he has in fact changed pace for a stride or two.

Firm rules: Any rider whose pony breaks into a faster pace than the one specified must stop and turn a circle before continuing.

Chase Me Charlie

Objective: To negotiate two jumps without knocking them down, refusing or running out, while the height of the jumps rises with each round.

Equipment: Two jumps, with extra poles and fillers available, set up on opposite sides of the arena.

Method: Riders follow one another round the arena, without crowding.

Drawbacks: With two or more good ponies taking part, the jumps may get higher than is really safe by the end of the contest. Riders should be encouraged to divide the placings if the jumps have risen to four feet without a decision being reached.

Firm rules: A rider failing to negotiate a jump must leave the arena immediately.

Dressing-up Race

Objective: To ride to the end of the arena, don various items of dress and return to the finishing line.
Equipment for each lane: Three or more items of clothing such as a shirt, pyjama trousers, scarf, etc., laid out on an upturned bin or hung on a pole.
Method: Each competitor rides to the clothes, dons them and returns to the finish. The organiser should make it clear at the start whether the rider is obliged to dismount or not. If trousers are not included in the selection, dismounting may not be necessary.
Firm rules: If buttons are to be done up, make certain that all competitors are aware of the fact.

Eating and Drinking Race

Objective: To eat a biscuit and drink a beaker of water before returning to the finish.
Equipment for each lane: Upturned bin on which is placed a dry biscuit and a plastic beaker half-filled with water.
Method: Rider canters to bin, dismounts, eats the biscuit, drinks the water and returns to the finish.
Drawbacks: Unless a steward is stationed at each bin, it is hard to monitor the eating and drinking. It is also not very hygienic if the same beakers are used for each heat.
Firm rules: If the beaker is accidentally knocked over before the water is drunk, the rider is eliminated.

Egg and Spoon Race

Objective: To carry an egg, either hard-boiled or artificial, in a spoon for a specified distance without touching the egg with the hand.
Equipment for each lane: Metal or plastic spoon. Hard-boiled egg or wooden egg. Line of bending poles or marker cone at far end of the arena.
Method: There are two ways of running this race. In the first, the rider is handed the egg and spoon at the start; she then bends

up the line of bending poles and back again, steering her pony with one hand and holding the spoon with the other. In the second, the competitor rides round the marker and back to the centre line, where a spoon with the egg beside it has been placed on the ground. She dismounts, picks up the spoon, scoops up the egg and leads her pony to the finish.

Firm rules: If the egg is dropped, it must be replaced and the race continued from the point where the error occurred. In the first version, a rider may hold the egg with her hand while she is remounting.

Fishing Race

Objective: To transfer plastic or wooden 'fish' from 'pond' to 'larder'.

Equipment for each lane: Three or four fish-shaped pieces of wood or plastic, about fifteen inches (thirty-eight centimetres) long and seven-and-a-half inches (nineteen centimetres) wide; each fish should have a ring in its nose. Open litter bin on centre lane to form the 'pond' into which the fish are placed. T-shaped post, four feet (1.2 metres) high, with hooks attached to the underside of the crosspiece, fixed in the ground at the far end, or held by a steward. Piece of dowelling, three feet (ninety centimetres) long, with a small hook at one end; this represents the fishing rod.

Method: Carrying the fishing rod, the rider gallops to the bin, hooks out a fish and races to the larder, the post at the far end. There, she detaches the fish from the rod and hangs it on one of the hooks on the crosspiece. She then repeats the operation with the remaining fish. When all the fish have been caught, she rides to the finish.

Firm rules: If a fish is dropped, the rider should dismount to retrieve it and may hook it to the fishing rod before remounting and continuing. If it falls while she is trying to hang it on the crosspiece, she may dismount to get it but should be back on her pony before hanging it on its hook. If the 'pond' is upset, the rider must set it up again and replace any spilled fish.

Five Flag Race

Objective: To transfer flags from one cone to another.

Equipment for each lane: Two cones, one on the far line, one on the centre line. The latter cone contains four flags. A fifth flag is given to the rider at the start. Each flag consists of a four-foot (1.2-metre) bamboo cane with a 'flag' of coloured material attached to one end.

Method: Carrying a flag, the rider gallops to the far end and deposits it in the empty cone. She then collects the flags one at a time from the other cone. The last flag should be carried to the finish.

Firm rules: Flags must be collected singly. If two flags are picked up accidentally, one must be replaced before the other is transferred. Fallen cones and flags must be set up properly before the rider continues the race, but if she has to dismount in order to do this she may place the flag in the cone from the ground.

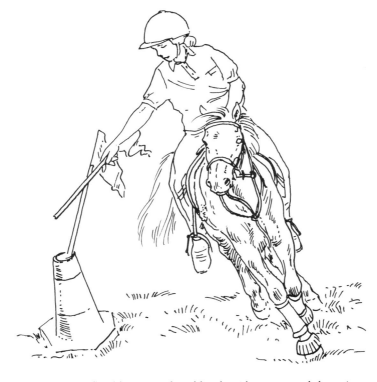

Holding the flag like a sword enables the rider to control the point, thus making it easier to insert it into the cane.

Gretna Green (for pairs)

Objective: One rider is the 'groom', the other is the 'bride'. The groom collects his bride and carries her to the finish.

Equipment for each lane: Four bending poles.

Method One: Rider One bends up the line of poles to the far end where Rider Two is waiting: Rider Two gets up on the pony behind Rider One and they both bend back to the finish.

Method Two: Played as above except that Rider Two is mounted. When the 'bride' is joined by her partner, the two riders clasp hands and together bend through the poles to the finish.

Firm rules: Should the pair let go of each other before crossing the finishing line, they must resume the race at the point where the error occurred. They must also return if a pole is missed out. A broken pole or a pole knocked right out of the ground means elimination.

Hi-Lo Race

Objective: To transfer tennis balls from a row of cones to a net on the top of a pole.

Equipment for each lane: Four cones in a line, each holding a tennis ball. A fifth ball which is given to the rider. A pole at the far end of the arena. A net on a ring eight inches (twenty centimetres) in diameter attached to a pole seven feet (2.1 metres) tall. This pole may be fixed in the ground or, if necessary, held by a steward.

Method: The rider, carrying a ball, gallops to the pole and deposits the ball in the net. She then collects the remaining tennis balls in turn from the cones and places them in the net before returning to the finish.

Firm rules: Fallen cones must be replaced and dropped balls retrieved before the rider continues the race.

Jelly Baby Gobble

Objective: To collect a jelly baby or similar sweet from a plate containing a small heap of flour.

Equipment for each lane: Plate with a rim. Small quantity of flour in the centre of the plate. Jelly baby projecting slightly from the flour. Cone or pole at far end of arena.

Method: Rider gallops to far end, goes round marker and returns to the plate. She dismounts and retrieves the jelly baby with her teeth before riding to the finish.

Drawbacks: On a windy day, the flour may be blown off the plate and this race is possibly best confined to gymkhanas held in indoor arenas.

Firm rules: The jelly baby must not be touched by the rider's hand. If the rider upsets the plate on her way up the arena, she is eliminated.

Knickerbocker Glory

Objective: To carry an 'ice-cream cone' up and down a line of bending poles.

Equipment for each lane: Line of four or five bending poles. 'Ice-cream cone', formed by cutting off the top of a road cone. Plastic ball, six inches (fifteen centimetres) in diameter.

Method: The rider must balance the ball on the cup of the cone and bend up and back through the line of bending poles.

Firm rules: The rider may not touch the ball with her hand or hold it in place. If the ball is dropped, she must dismount and retrieve it and hold it in position until she is ready to resume the race. If she misses a pole, she must return to that point before continuing.

Litter Race – One

Objective: To collect litter on the end of a cane and place it in a litter bin.

Equipment for each lane: Between three and five pieces of litter at the far end of the arena. Swingbin, without lid, on the centre line. Bamboo cane, four feet (1.2 metres) long. The litter comprises plastic one-litre washing-up liquid containers, cut off at the shoulder.

Method: The rider uses the cane to pick up each piece of litter in turn and deposit it in the litter bin. When all the litter is in the bin, she rides to the finish.

Drawbacks: This is quite a difficult race for inexperienced riders, although members of a Prince Philip squad will have few problems. If the race is included in an ordinary gymkhana, be prepared for a lot of frustrated competitors and a race which will take a long time to complete.

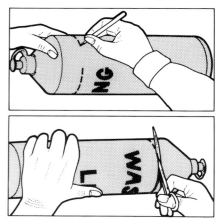

Firm rules: The litter may only be picked up by hand if it misses the bin while the rider is trying to deposit it or if the bin and its contents are accidentally knocked over. In the latter case, the bin must be replaced before the rider continues.

Litter Race – Two

Objective: Similar to Litter Race – One but timing plays an important part.

Equipment for each lane: Swingbin on start line, open end up. Ten to fifteen pieces of litter (washing-up liquid containers prepared as above) at far end of arena. Bamboo cane, as above.

Method: Rider uses cane to collect as many pieces of litter as she can in, say, one to two minutes, depositing each piece in turn in the bin. A whistle is blown when time is up, and stewards then count the number of pieces in each bin.

Drawbacks: Skilled riders tend to collect the same amount of litter in the time allowed, which means that no clear winner emerges. This game was devised for Pony Club mounted games, with team members working in pairs to pick up litter. It was soon found that there was not enough difference in skill between the teams to give a proper result and the points awarded for the placings had therefore to be divided. It has not been used in the Prince Philip competition for some years.

Firm rules: Bins accidentally knocked over must be righted and fallen litter replaced before the race continues. This may be done from the ground.

Moat and Castle

Objective: To transfer a tennis ball from a bucket of water (the moat) to a cone (the castle).
Equipment for each lane: Bucket half-filled with water on central line. Cone at far end. Two tennis balls floating in the water.
Method: Rider gallops to bucket and collects one of the balls, dismounting if necessary. She then remounts, rides to cone and leaves the ball on top, collecting the second ball on the way back.
Firm rules: Riders are not obliged to dismount when gathering the ball, but if they do so they must remount before transferring it to the cone. Fallen equipment must be replaced. If all the water is spilled, the rider is eliminated.

Mug Race – One

Objective: To transfer mugs from an upturned bin to the tops of bending poles.
Equipment for each lane: Line of four bending poles. Inverted swingbin at far end of arena. Four metal mugs with handles placed inverted on the bin. Fifth mug to be given to the rider at the start.
Method: Rider takes the first mug and places it on top of one of the poles. She then collects three more in turn and puts one on each of the remaining poles. Finally she collects the remaining mug and rides to the finish.
Firm rules: Fallen mugs must be retrieved and put back on the pole or on the bin, although the rider need not remount before doing so. If the mug is being returned to the bin, it must be inverted as before.

Mug Race – Two

Objective: To transfer metal mugs from one pole to another.
Equipment for each lane: Four bending poles. Three metal mugs with handles inverted on the top of the first three poles.
Method: Competitor rides to Pole Three, collects mug and places it on Pole Four. She then transfers the mugs on Poles One and Two to Poles Two and Three. When all three mugs have been moved

The Mug Race: keep your reins short so that the pony is totally under control while you are placing the mug on top of the pole.

and are safely on their new poles, she rides to the finish.
Firm rules: Fallen mugs must be picked up at once, but may be placed on the appropriate pole from the ground.

Musical Mats

Objective: To reach and stand on a mat when the music stops before anyone else. Note: this event is not run in lanes.
Equipment: Several plastic or hessian sacks, at least as many as the number of entries. Cones to mark out the perimeter of a circle. Music – or, if this is not possible, whistle or hooter which can be heard across the arena.
Method: Riders follow one another round the circle. When the music stops or the whistle sounds, they must immediately dismount and lead their ponies to the sacks. Note to organisers: it is a good idea to have a sack for everyone in the first – trial – round to make certain that everyone understands the rules. Thereafter, remove one sack at a time until one rider – the winner – is left.
Firm rules: Riders must dismount as soon as the music stops. In

the event of a dispute between two riders as to which of them reached a mat first, do not remove a mat but run the round again.

Musical Statues

Objective: To stand perfectly still when the music stops and not move until told to do so. No lanes.
Equipment: Cones to mark perimeter of a circle. Music.
Method: Riders follow one another round the circle, stopping as soon as the music stops. Any rider or pony moving at this point is eliminated. Remaining riders move on when the music starts again. Judges have to be very strict in this game, eliminating ponies for swishing tails or tossing heads.
Drawbacks: It is hard to be fair in this game as a large number of competitors get eliminated early on and the best, the last two or three, are so still that they are almost impossible to separate. However, this game is quite suitable for very young leading-rein riders or severely disabled riders.

Musical Wands

Objective: To avoid being eliminated when the music stops for failing to reach a pole with a beaker on top.
Equipment: Several bending poles randomly placed within the perimeter of a circle marked by cones. Plastic beakers or cups on all or some of the poles (depending on the number of entries). Music.
Method: This game is similar to Musical Mats except that riders do not have to dismount before going into the centre of the circle. When competitors have had one trial round in which no one is eliminated, one of the beakers is removed (there is no need to take down the pole as well), the music restarts and the riders return to the outside of the circle. Beakers are removed before each round until only one is left.
Safety note: When only two riders are left, it is customary to send them round the circle on opposite reins. Organisers should ensure that the music stops when the two riders are just passing each other so that they race for the final beaker side by side. If the music stops when they are on opposite sides, both riders may be so intent on reaching the beaker that they collide, running the risk of serious injury to both them and their ponies.

113

Obstacle Race

Any number from two to five games can be combined for this race; the choice lies with the organisers. Briefing needs to be carried out with care.

Pony Club Race

Objective: To hang eight letters on hooks on a frame or 'gallows' in the correct order, so that the words PONY CLUB are spelt out.

Equipment for each lane: Inverted bin on centre line on which eight letters are stacked in random order. Post, measuring seven feet (2.1 metres) high, with two crossbars, at the far end. Each crossbar has four hooks screwed to the lower edge. The letters are painted on to square pieces of hardboard and a ring attached to the top edge of each piece. This game was devised by the Pony Club as a team game, which is why the words PONY CLUB were selected. Other words could be chosen, provided they are easily recognised and spelt. The post, or gallows, needs to be securely fixed into the ground; if this is not possible, a steward should be detailed to hold it.

Method: The rider gallops to the letters, selects two, then rides to the gallows and hangs them in their correct position on the crossbars. She returns to the bin three further times until all the letters have been collected and hung up. She then rides to the finish. She may pick two letters at random when visiting the bin or take the time to choose the letters in their proper order. Either way, the finished display should spell the words correctly.

Firm rules: Fallen equipment must be retrieved or set up again properly. If a letter falls while in the process of being attached to its hook, the competitor should dismount to pick it up but must remount before again attempting to place it in position. Stewards holding the gallows may not assist the riders in any way.

Post Office Race

Objective: To collect three or four letters and post them into a letter box.

Equipment for each lane: Cardboard box with a lid in which a rectangular slit measuring six inches by two inches (fifteen centimetres by five centimetres) has been cut. Table or up-turned bin on which the box is placed at the far end of the arena. Four bending poles with an envelope attached by means of a rubber band to the top of each.

Method: Rider gallops up the line of bending poles, collects a letter and posts it in the box. She then repeats the process with the remaining letters before returning to the finish.

Firm rules: Letters may be collected in any order and, if dropped, must be retrieved before the next letter is collected. If the box falls, that too must be set up again before the rider continues the race. When all the letters have been posted, the rider returns to the finish.

Potato Race

Played in the same way as Ball and Bucket, using potatoes instead of tennis balls (see page 99).

Pyramid Race

Objective: To transfer plastic ice-cream cartons from one table to another.

Equipment for each lane: Four square ice-cream containers, weighted with sand and with sealed lids, placed side by side on a table at the far end of the arena. Similar table on centre line.

Method: Rider gallops to far end, collects a carton and places it on the centre table. She then collects the remaining three in turn, stacking them one at a time on top of the first. When the pyramid is complete, she rides to the finish.

Firm rules: Fallen cartons must be picked up and the table recovered if it is knocked over.

Ring Race

Objective: To transfer a number of rings from a gallows to a bending pole.

Equipment for each lane: Post with a crosspiece at the far end of the arena. Five rubber vacuum cleaner rings, four of which

By keeping her reins short, this rider has close control over her pony – essential when trying to place a carton on top of another in the Pyramid Race.

are hanging on cup hooks screwed to the underside of the crosspiece. Bending pole.

Method: Rider starts with a ring and gallops up the arena, depositing the ring over the bending pole en route. She then collects each of the remaining four rings in turn and places them over the pole. When all five rings are in place, she rides to the finish.

Firm rules: A fallen ring must be picked up immediately. Rider should remount before placing it on the pole.

Sack Race

Objective: To reach the winning post first whilst shuffling in a sack and leading the pony.

Equipment for each race: Marker cone at the far end. Hessian sack placed on the centre line, with the open end towards the start.

Sack Race. The rider holds the sack up to her waist, keeping contact with her pony with her right hand.

Method: Each rider races round the marker cone and back to the sack, where she dismounts, gets into the sack and, leading her pony by the reins, shuffles or jumps to the finish.

Firm rules: A rider must hold the sack above her knees and stay in it until both she and her pony are across the finishing line. She may not lean on her pony's neck or withers in order to get a 'lift' whilst moving in the sack.

Saddling-up Race

Objective: After starting the race bareback, to saddle up and return to the finish.

Equipment for each lane: None.

Method: Before the start, the rider removes her saddle and places it on the ground at the far end of the arena. She then returns to the starting line and mounts. At the starting signal, she rides bareback to her saddle, dismounts and saddles up, remounting for the gallop back to the finish.

Drawbacks: Organisers may feel that this race is unfair to those riders whose ponies wear martingales.

Firm rules: The saddle must be in its proper position with both girth buckles fastened. The rider must have her feet in the stirrups before crossing the finishing line.

Shoe Scramble

Objective: To find a matching shoe hidden in a pile of straw.
Equipment: Two or three bales of straw scattered in a pile at the far end of the arena. A different pair of shoes for each lane. One shoe from each pair is hidden in the straw; its partner is held by a steward at the far end of every lane.
Method: The rider gallops to the steward and dismounts. Handing her pony to the steward, she receives a shoe and then goes to the straw to find its partner. When she has a pair she returns to her pony, hands the shoes to the steward and rides to the finish.
Note to organisers: Care must be taken to select pairs of shoes that are noticeably different. This is a good event to have in a show dominated by skilled gymkhana performers as the less skilled competitors often emerge the winners.

Shopping Race

Objective: To complete a shopping list by visiting several 'shops' in turn and getting a signature from the 'shopkeeper'.
Equipment: Cone or post in the centre of a circle, where the judge is positioned. Nine posts spaced out round the perimeter of the circle, each bearing the name of a shop – Fishmonger, Butcher, Baker, etc. Shopping lists – cards with the names of the shops in a different order for each card and a space beside each shop for a signature (there should be enough cards for each competitor to be given one). Pencil, with spare, for each shopkeeper (stewards).
Method: A steward stands at each of the posts with pencil in hand. Each rider is given a shopping list and then proceeds to work down the list, collecting a signature from each shopkeeper in turn. The shops must be visited in the order they appear on the card. As soon as a card is completed, the rider takes it to the judge in the centre for scrutiny. The first to arrive at the judge with her card correctly filled in is the winner.
Drawbacks: This is quite a complicated game both to set up and explain, but it is different from the usual run of races, does

not require heats and gives an equal chance to skilled and unskilled riders.

Firm rules: If a rider arrives at a shop in the wrong order, the steward should not sign her card but direct her to the correct shop.

Sock and Bucket

See Ball and Bucket (page 99).

Spillers Pole Race

Objective: To drop plastic cylinders, each inscribed with a letter, over a bending pole so that when all are in place the word SPILLERS can be read from top to bottom.

Equipment for each lane: Bending pole on centre line. Eight washing-up liquid containers with the tops and bottoms cut off, leaving a cylinder measuring six inches (fifteen centimetres). Each cylinder is clearly marked with one of the letters of the word SPILLERS. The cylinders are placed on the ground at the

The Spillers Pole Race. As soon as the final letter is in position, the rider will be off, as hard as she can, to the finish.

end of the arena except for the one bearing the letter S, which is
given to the rider at the start.

Method: The rider gallops to the pole and drops the cylinder
over it, making certain that the S is the right way up. She then
collects each of the cylinders in turn from the far end and drops
them over the pole, taking care to get them in the right order.

Firm rules: Letters put in the wrong order must be sorted. The
rider will have to dismount to do this but must remount before
crossing the finishing line.

Note to organisers: If there are a large number of competitors
for this event and several heats, it can be speeded up by giving
the riders two cylinders to start with and requesting them to
collect the others two at a time.

Stepping-Stone Dash

Objective: To run across a row of stepping-stones, leading the
pony, without falling off.

Equipment for each lane: Marker cone at the end of the arena.
Six blocks or upturned flowerpots set at right angles to and

Negotiating the flowerpots in the Stepping-Stone Dash. Riders are
not allowed to lean on their ponies while moving across the stones.

across the centre line, forming the stepping-stones. They should be two feet (sixty centimetres) apart.

Method: The rider gallops round the marker and back to the stepping-stones where she dismounts, runs across the stones without falling off or missing one out, remounts and rides to the finish.

Firm rules: Should a rider fall off or miss a stone, she must return to the first stone and start again.

Sword Race

Objective: To collect four rings on the end of a wooden sword.

Equipment for each lane: Cone at far end of arena. Line of four bending poles, with a metal or plastic ring attached to the top of each post with a rubber band. The rings should have an internal diameter of four inches (ten centimetres) and a short stem for fixing to the pole. Wooden sword, two feet (sixty centimetres) long, with a hilt measuring twelve inches (thirty centimetres) fixed across the sword nine inches (twenty-three centimetres) from one end. The sword is placed point downwards in the cone.

Method: The rider gallops to the cone, collects the sword and gallops back to the finish, collecting the four rings on the way.

Firm rules: The rider is not allowed to touch the blade of the sword. Fallen rings, however, may be picked up and put on the sword by hand and held in place while the rider remounts. Once back in the saddle, the sword must again be held by the handle.

Triple Flag Race

Objective: To transfer three different coloured flags from a single cone and place them in three separate cones.

Equipment for each lane: Cone at the far end containing three flags, each a different colour. Three empty cones at the start end in line with the first bending pole. Each cone should clearly correspond with one of the flags at the other end by having a tape or ribbon around it, matching the colour of the flag.

Method: The rider gallops to the far end, collects a flag and places it in the empty cone bearing a tape of the same colour. The remaining flags are then collected one at a time in the same way.

Firm rules: The flags must be in their correct cones. If a mistake is made, it need not be corrected until all three flags have been brought back to the start end, but they must be right before the rider crosses the finishing line. Fallen flags and cones must, however, be righted straight away.

Trotting Race

Objective: To win the race at a trot without breaking into a canter.
Equipment for each lane: Marker cone at far end.
Method: Each competitor trots to the marker, turns round it and trots to the finish.
Firm rules: If the pony breaks into a canter, even for only one stride, the rider must circle before continuing.
Note to organisers: As with any race where changes of pace earn an instant penalty, the race is difficult for one judge to referee. Because it requires so little equipment it is a popular choice for gymkhanas, but it can cause ill-feeling unless a separate steward is appointed to each lane with instructions to monitor the pony's actions and see that he circles at the first sign of a break.

Tyre Race

Objective: To get through a tyre and back to the finish in the shortest time.
Equipment for each lane: Lightweight motorcycle tyre at the far end.
Method: Rider gallops to the tyre, dismounts, gets through it, remounts and rides to the finish.
Firm rules: When wriggling through the tyre, the rider must keep hold of her pony at all times, transferring the reins to the other hand when necessary.

Unsaddling Race

Objective: To ride to a point, remove the saddle and ride bareback to the finish.
Equipment for each lane: Marker cone at far end.

A team event – the Tyre Race. The rider has negotiated the tyre without mishap and now vaults back in the saddle. Her partner will not let go of the pony until she is sure that his rider is back in control.

Method: Rider gallops to the cone, dismounts, runs up stirrups and removes saddle, placing it on the ground. She then remounts and rides bareback to the finish.

Firm rules: The stirrup irons must be securely run up. If they are not, the rider must return to her saddle to correct the error before continuing. She must be astride her pony before crossing the finishing line.

VC Race

Objective: To rescue a 'wounded comrade'.

Equipment for each lane: Line of four bending poles. Hessian or paper sack, loosely filled with hay or straw and secured at the top, placed on the ground at the far end.

Method: The rider bends up the bending poles, collects the sack and, placing it across the pommel of her saddle, bends back to the finish.

Firm rules: An error, such as a missed pole, must be corrected before continuing. The sack may be picked up without dismounting.

Walk and Trot

Objective: To walk to the far end and trot back to the finish without altering pace.

Equipment for each lane: Marker cone at far end.

Method: Rider walks to the cone, turns around it and trots back to the finish.

Firm rules: Rider must circle her pony if he moves up into another pace.

Note to organisers: As with Canter, Trot and Walk (see page 104) and Trotting Race (see page 122), this is a difficult race to monitor fairly without having a separate judge for each lane.

Walk, Trot and Canter

Objective: Similar to above, except that the trotting phase is increased to two lengths of the arena and the final length from marker cone to finish is covered at a gallop.

Equipment for each lane: Marker cone at far end.

Note to organisers: Some people feel that the dash to the finish could be dangerous unless there is plenty of room between the finishing line and the perimeter ropes because some children may have difficulty in pulling up. However, this is a criticism that can be levelled at a number of games. The answer is that, when setting up the arena, organisers should ensure a wide pulling-up space.

Water Race

Objective: To transfer water from one end of the arena to the other.

Equipment for each lane: Large upturned bin or container such as an oil drum at the far end. Upturned bin at the starting end. Bucket of water placed on the oil drum and empty twelve-ounce (340 gram) coffee jar or plastic ice-cream container on the bin. Plastic beaker or metal mug to be handed to the rider at the start. Stopwatch and whistle. Measuring jug.

Method: Rider gallops to bucket and fills her mug with water. She carries this back to the jar or carton and tips it in before returning for another load. After a specified length of time (one-and-a-half or two minutes), the whistle is blown and the rider immediately stops unless she is in the act of emptying her beaker into the jar. The judge then moves down the line of jars, using the measuring jug to calculate the amount of water in each jar. *Firm rules*: If a jar is knocked over, it can be righted by a steward. A steward may similarly restore a fallen bucket, refilling it with water. However, either occurrence effectively loses the rider the race, since the winner is the rider whose jar contains the most water.

Note to organisers: This is quite a good race for riders with steady ponies which can be controlled easily with one hand. Two five-gallon containers of water are needed so that one can be stationed at each side.

Chapter Three
Making Equipment

Whether you need equipment for practising or because you are organising a gymkhana, it is possible to make most of it at home.

Almost all the games in popular use require items which are reasonably easy to acquire and neither difficult nor expensive to make.

Things to Buy

Cones

These *have* to be bought. However tempting it may be to remove cones from the highway, this is illegal and could be dangerous. Cones are not very expensive and can be bought from suppliers of road-mending equipment and some builders' merchants. They are available in varying sizes, but the most useful measures two feet (sixty centimetres) from top to bottom.

Provided they are looked after, they will last many years. Cones deteriorate if they are left out of doors in the winter when the plastic material from which they are made becomes brittle in frosty conditions. Usually it is the base which fails. The base is hollow and filled with sand to weigh it down and give it the necessary stability. If the plastic cracks and the sand trickles out, the cone can easily be knocked over or blown over in a strong wind.

Cones are stored by stacking them one on the other. They are quite heavy and only about six to eight can be carried in one go.

The versatility of cones has made them ideal gymkhana equipment. The top inch of a cone will have to be cut off to enable a tennis ball to be balanced on it, but it can still be used as a marker. Broom handles can be inserted in these small holes to create bending poles.

For a flag-holder, the cone must be cut off about halfway down so that the hole measures four inches (ten centimetres) in diameter. To ensure that each cone is similar and the cut is made in the right place, it is necessary to make a collar for the cone.

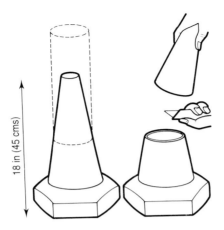

Use a strip of paper or thin card, measuring twelve-and-a-half inches (thirty-two centimetres) long; staple or stick the ends together. If you place the collar over the cone, you can mark a cutting line round the cone at the bottom edge of the collar.

Use a sharp knife, such as a Stanley knife, whenever you have to cut a cone. It is quite hard to do but after tackling a few cones you will learn the knack. It is worth retaining the top half of the cone as it makes a perfect holder, inverted, for the Knickerbocker Glory race.

Balls

These also *have* to be bought. The most versatile balls are tennis balls – look out for cheap offers in local sports shops. If you are planning to organise a gymkhana you will need several, and if you choose you can make them a different colour for each lane by dunking them in a cold-water dye.

Tennis balls are usually available in white or yellow. Use a blue dye to turn white balls into blue ones and yellow ones to green ones. Use a red dye to make pink/red and orange balls. Giving the pink/red balls the blue dye treatment will produce lilac or purple ones. Thus, with only two dyes, you finish up with a different coloured set of balls for each of seven lanes.

Plastic beach balls can be bought quite cheaply. Those measuring six inches (fifteen centimetres) are the most suitable for the Knickerbocker Glory race, but if you feel the children taking part are likely to be too good you can make the race more difficult by buying larger beach balls.

Soft, foam rubber balls, of the type sold with a child's tennis set, have their uses, particularly in the Aunt Sally game. The Pony Club game Polocrosse uses foam rubber balls measuring twelve inches (thirty centimetres) in circumference.

Balloons

These, of course, cannot be used again since the object of the Balloon Race is to burst the balloon. Packets of balloons are cheap to buy. However, unless you have lots of puff, it is worth investing in a balloon pump.

Canes

Any garden centre can sell you bamboo canes. The size most commonly used for all manner of gymkhana games is four feet (1.2 metres) in length. Canes form the basis for flags and are necessary for the Balloon Race and the Litter Race.

The drawback of bamboo is that it has a tendency to split at the ends. This can be largely prevented by strapping the ends with insulating tape. Here again, with the variously coloured tape on the market, you can colour-code the canes for each lane.

Buckets

These essential items of equipment for any gymkhana do, of course, have the added advantage that they can be used for other

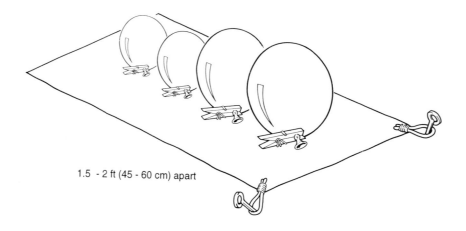

1.5 - 2 ft (45 - 60 cm) apart

purposes when not needed for the games. Many organisers, however, like to keep games buckets separate from the ones used in your stable yard. There is nothing more annoying at the start of a show than to find that half your buckets are missing.

Mugs and Beakers

Camping shops sell the type of mug used in Pony Club Prince Philip Cup games. These are made of metal and are fitted with handles. A circlet of insulating tape just under the rim will identify the mugs as yours, or colour-code them if you wish. Plastic beakers without handles are available at hardware shops. These are necessary where the rules of a game require the mugs to be stacked. Plastic disposable cups are useful for a game such as Musical Wands. They are very light, however, and can blow away in a strong wind. They also split quite easily.

Bins

Bins with swing lids are the best size and are very versatile. Most big do-it-yourself stores sell them and it is not necessary to buy the lids. Right way up, the bins can be used as containers; inverted, they are useful as tables. Table tops can be made by a handyman to fit into the open end of the bins.

Things to save

Old socks

Never let anyone in your home throw away socks. You can never have too many, especially as they are the easiest things to lose during training or at a show. Keep a carrier bag handy into which old socks can be dumped. You will than have a supply to draw upon when you need them.

Remnants

Scraps of material can be used to make flags. If the scraps are not big enough, it may be necessary to visit a soft furnishings or fabrics shop at sale time to see what is available in the way of end-of-roll material and other remnants.

Bottles

Plastic one-litre squash bottles form the basis of some games. Save standard bottles of similar shape and make certain they still have

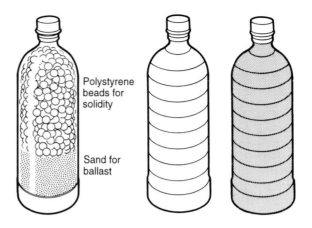

their screw tops. Half-fill each bottle with sand to weight it and give it stability. Top up with polystyrene beads to prevent the bottle from squashing when being handled. If you want to paint the bottles in bright colours, it is important to bind each bottle with adhesive tape first. Paint applied directly to the bottle makes the plastic brittle, causing it to split when being used.

Cartons

Ice-cream cartons with snap-on lids have numerous uses. The best ones to save are the square ones. Washing-up liquid containers, the one-litre size, are needed for the Litter Race and the Spillers Pole Race. The important ones are the taller type, not the ones containing concentrated liquid. You will need a large number so spread the word around all your friends and relations. It takes quite a time to build up a collection.

Clothing

All manner of old clothing can be saved but, if you are collecting for a show, ensure that you have enough shirts or pyjama jackets of a similar size. Hats and mufflers need not be identical. Old shoes, for the Shoe Scramble, must be varied in colour and design and should be in pairs.

Sacks

Hessian sacks are best for the Sack Race but have become increasingly difficult to obtain. If you are offered any, never turn them down. Paper sacks have been substituted for hessian ones but they are useless if the weather is wet. Plastic sacks can be used in Musical Mats.

Tyres

Old tyres should not be hard to find, but it may take a while to collect together enough tyres of the same size. Look for motorcycle and bicycle tyres, not car tyres, which are too big and heavy.

Things to make

Flags

These are made from scraps of material and it is easier if you have a sewing-machine at your disposal. Decide how big you want your flag to be, add half an inch (1.5 centimetres) hem allowance to all dimensions and make a template out of newspaper. One end of the flag needs to have a hem wide enough to take a bamboo cane and the top edge of this hem should be stitched across. To keep the flag safely on the cane, slip it over the end and secure the lower part with insulating tape.

Bending poles

Because of the number required for the average show, poles represent any show organiser's most expensive purchase. Even when you are making them yourself, they are not cheap. The easiest to acquire are broom handles, which provide poles of the right height. Alternatively, lengths of softwood (one inch by one inch – 2.5 centimetres by 2.5 centimetres – or slightly thicker if more substantial poles are required) can be bought at any timber merchants. The softwood should be cut to size and each pole, whether broom handle or softwood, must be tapered at one end. Poles can be left bare, varnished, or painted in bright colours to make them readily visible. Do *not* use canes or metal fencing stakes for bending poles as both are dangerous. It is best to have at least forty poles for the average show so that there is always a spare one available if a pole gets broken. If the ground is very hard, poles may be supported in cones, but you will then need to have a large quantity of cones which have not been cut down.

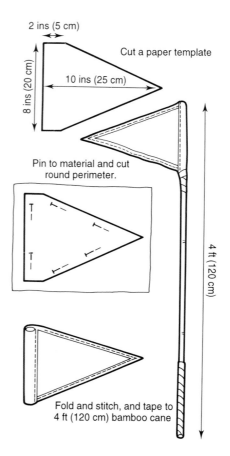

2 ins (5 cm)

Cut a paper template

8 ins (20 cm)

10 ins (25 cm)

Pin to material and cut round perimeter.

4 ft (120 cm)

Fold and stitch, and tape to 4 ft (120 cm) bamboo cane

Sock missiles

To turn an old sock into an effective missile for the Aunt Sally game, or to be used in Sock and Bucket, you need something more substantial than simply rolling it up will provide. A little extra care in the preparation will make the socks last. Stuff the toe of the sock with screwed-up newspaper before rolling up and secure the end by stitching. If possible try to collect brightly coloured socks as these will show up when they are on the ground, especially if the grass is long.

Toe of sock stuffed with crumpled newspaper

Roll up sock

Stitch up end

Letter boxes

Used in the Post Office Race, the best boxes are the type which once contained five reams of typing or copy paper. They are usually fairly substantial and have a snug-fitting lid. Friends who work in an office can no doubt obtain the boxes for you. Cut a slit in the box lid to the appropriate size. The boxes make excellent storage containers for small items such as socks, mugs, tennis balls, etc.

Gallows

This term is generally used to describe the post and crosspieces necessary for the Pony Club Race and Fishing Race. To be sure that a gallows lasts, it is best to mortise the joints properly, and it is wise to borrow the services of a handyman if you do not feel confident that you can do the job yourself. Lengths of softwood measuring one inch by two inches (2.5 centimetres by five

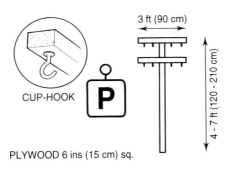

CUP-HOOK

P

PLYWOOD 6 ins (15 cm) sq.

3 ft (90 cm)

4 - 7 ft (120 - 210 cm)

133

centimetres) are required. In the Pony Club Race, the crosspiece is fixed four feet (1.2 metres) from the ground; in the Pony Club Race, the crosspieces are between fifteen and twenty-one inches (37.5 and 52.5 centimetres) apart, with the top one seven feet (2.1 metres) from the ground. The crosspieces in all cases are three feet (ninety centimetres) long and have cuphooks screwed to the underside at intervals of just under one foot (thirty centimetres).

Tabletops

If you feel that the horizontal surface provided by an upturned bin is not big enough for your purpose, it will be necessary to make tabletops to fit inside the open end of the bins. They can be made from three-quarter-inch (1.8-centimetre) blockboard, compression board or laminated chipboard. When cut to size, each top should have small blocks attached to the underside so that it will fit snugly into the bin.

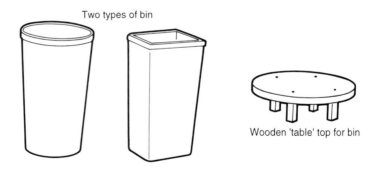

Two types of bin

Wooden 'table' top for bin

Speciality items

Swords

Wooden swords take a little time to make properly, but with care will last. Each sword needs a four-foot (1.2-metre) length of one inch by one inch softwood. Mark off one foot (thirty centimetres) from one end and cut the wood in two at this point. The shorter piece will form the crosspiece and is fixed across the longer piece one foot (thirty centimetres) from the

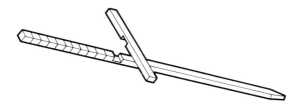

end. Cut the joint so that the crosspiece is flush with the sword. Use a plane to taper the blade and to round off the angles. Finish with sandpaper. If you like, the sword can be painted and the handle bound with insulating tape.

Tennis racquets
Old-style racquets with a wooden frame are the easiest to adapt, as a crosspiece needs to be fixed to the handle so that it projects three inches (7.5 centimetres) on each side. The purpose of the crosspiece is to provide an easily recognisable point in front of which the rider's hand is not allowed to stray.

Rings
The rings used for the Sword Race are quite difficult to make accurately unless you have metal-working equipment available. The internal diameter of each ring should be four inches (ten centimetres) and the overall diameter six inches (fifteen centimetres). Each ring should have a short stem so that it can be attached to the top of a

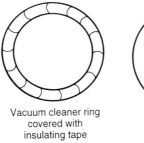

Vacuum cleaner ring
covered with
insulating tape

Ring for Sword Race

bending pole. If you feel that it would be too difficult to make at home, prepare a template in cardboard and take it to a blacksmith, who would be able to cut it out for you in sheet metal.

For the Ring Race, you need vacuum cleaner rings, which are made of rubber and are readily available at shops selling household appliances. They are usually black and can be quite difficult to see, but this problem can be remedied by binding them in brightly coloured insulating tape.

Stepping-stones

The most important feature of stepping-stones is that they should be stable even when placed on grass. Wooden blocks can be used. They should measure at least six inches by nine inches (fifteen centimetres by 22.5 centimetres) by four inches (ten centimetres) high. The Pony Club uses metal flowerpots for this race.

Storage

Equipment will last longer if it can be kept all together in a dry shed, preferably one that is fitted with shelves for smaller items. It can, of course, be stored in a corner of the tack room or barn, but things like buckets have a habit of being borrowed and not replaced if equipment is too accessible.

As you build up your collection, you will find that you become a popular choice as gymkhana judge at other people's shows. When you get invited, don't be surprised when, almost as an after-thought, you are asked to lend your equipment as well! Quite often, other organisers will only want your equipment and, for the sake of harmony in your neighbourhood, it is probably good policy to agree. Make certain, however, that every item is marked with your name – use indelible marker pens or white paint – and count the pieces out. The last thing you want when you come to run your own show is to find that you are short of vital equipment.

As a rule of thumb, the following table gives the quantity of items required for a show in which six rosettes are awarded for each race. All the figures allow for an extra lane if there are only seven competitors in a race, and spares are included in case of breakages.

Bending poles: four poles per lane plus two spares – 30
                     five poles per lane plus two spares – 35
Buckets: 7

Cones: cut-down for Flag Race – 14
            full height – 14
            spare ones for marking start and end lines – 4
Socks: four per lane plus two spares – 30
Tennis balls and potatoes: 30
Bottles: two per lane plus two spares – 16
Litter: at least 35 pieces
Canes: for Litter and Balloon races – 7
Balloons: at least 50
Rings: for Sword Race – 28
          for Ring Race with spares – 45
Sacks: for Sack Race – 8
          for Musical Mats – 30
Flags: five per lane – 35
Stepping-stones: 42
Clothing: at least 7 of each item
Shoes: for Shoe Scramble – 7 pairs
Ice-cream cartons: 28
Beach balls: 7
Cut-off tops of cones: for Knickerbocker Glory – 7
Letter boxes: 7
Letters: for Pony Club Race – 56 (7 of each letter)
Wooden fish: for Fishing Race – 28
Gallows: 7 of each type
Bins: 14
Table tops: 7

Supplier

All manner of gymkhana equipment can be bought from a supplier approved by the Pony Club.

The equipment is extremely colourful and efficient and the bending poles in particular are worth saving up for. This is because each pole is fitted with a metal spike and crosspiece for stamping it into the ground. A heavy metal base into which the spike can be slotted is available for each pole and is particularly useful when games are being held in a school with an all-weather or sand surface, when driving poles into the ground could damage the membrane on which the surface has been laid.

The company is very experienced in producing special items and are always up-to-date. For information on prices and to receive their catalogue, write to Quarry–Mech Ltd (QML); the address and telephone number are given in the Appendix.

Appendix

The following addresses could be useful to anyone wishing to join the Pony Club, obtain gymkhana equipment or order sweatshirts and other clothing.

* Write to Pony Club Headquarters for the name and address of the secretary of your nearest branch:
Pony Club Headquarters
British Horse Society
British Equestrian Centre
Stoneleigh
Kenilworth
Warwickshire CV8 2LR
Tel. 01203 696697

* Teenagers may be interested in the Mounted Games Association of Great Britain. Write to:
MGAGB
Europa Trading Estate
Parsonage Road
Stratton St Margaret
Swindon
Wiltshire SN3 4RJ
Tel. 01793 820709

* Catalogue and price list on gymkhana equipment can be obtained from:
Quarry-Mech Ltd (QML)
159 Churchfield Lane
Kexborough
Barnsley
S75 5DU
Tel. 01226 383805

* A wide range of sweatshirts and other clothing is available from:
Wainwright Promotions
Middle Street
Dewlish
Dorset DT2 7LX
Tel. 01258 837364
Fax 01258 837400

Index